Pictured on the front cover *(clockwise from top left):* Play Ball *(page 362),* Grilled Cheese & Turkey Shapes *(page 62),* Domino Cookies *(page 236)* and Funny Face Sandwich Melt *(page 46).*

Pictured on the back cover *(left to right):* Chicken Nuggets with Barbecue Dipping Sauce *(page 60),* Purple Cow Jumped Over the Moon *(page 100)* and Whip 'em Up Wacky Waffles *(page 6).*

ISBN: 0-7853-5427-1

Library of Congress Control Number: 2001094674

Manufactured in China.

8 7 6 5 4 3 2 1

Microwave Cooking: Microwave ovens vary in wattage. Use the cooking times as guidelines and check for doneness before adding more time.

Preparation/Cooking Times: Preparation times are based on the approximate amount of time required to assemble the recipe before cooking, baking, chilling or serving. These times include preparation steps such as measuring, chopping and mixing. The fact that some preparations and cooking can be done simultaneously is taken into account. Preparation of optional ingredients and serving suggestions is not included.

CONTENTS

BREAKFAST

oreo® muffins

1¾ cups all-purpose flour

½ cup sugar

1 tablespoon baking powder

½ teaspoon salt

¾ cup milk

⅓ cup sour cream

1 egg

¼ cup margarine or butter, melted

20 OREO® Chocolate Sandwich Cookies, coarsely chopped

1. Mix flour, sugar, baking powder and salt in medium bowl; set aside.

2. Blend milk, sour cream and egg in small bowl; stir into flour mixture with margarine or butter until just blended. Gently stir in cookie pieces. Spoon batter into 12 greased 2½-inch muffin-pan cups.

3. Bake at 400°F for 20 to 25 minutes or until toothpick inserted in center comes out clean. Remove from pan; cool on wire rack. Serve warm or cold.

makes 1 dozen muffins

whip 'em up wacky waffles

- 1½ cups biscuit baking mix
- 1 cup buttermilk
- 1 large egg
- 1 tablespoon vegetable oil
- ½ cup "M&M's"® Semi-Sweet Chocolate Mini Baking Bits
- Powdered sugar and maple syrup

Preheat Belgian waffle iron. In large bowl combine baking mix, buttermilk, egg and oil until well mixed. Spoon about ½ cup batter into hot waffle iron. Sprinkle with about 2 tablespoons "M&M's"® Semi-Sweet Chocolate Mini Baking Bits; top with about ½ cup batter. Close lid and bake until steaming stops, 1 to 2 minutes.* Sprinkle with powdered sugar and serve immediately with maple syrup and additional "M&M's"® Semi-Sweet Chocolate Mini Baking Bits. *makes 4 Belgian waffles*

Check the manufacturer's directions for recommended amount of batter and baking time.

chocolate waffles: Substitute 1¼ cups biscuit baking mix, ¼ cup unsweetened cocoa powder and ½ cup sugar for 1½ cups biscuit baking mix. Prepare and cook as directed above.

tip: These waffles make a great dessert too! Serve them with a scoop of ice cream, chocolate sauce and a sprinkle of "M&M's"® Chocolate Mini Baking Bits.

Don't open your waffle iron during the first minute of baking or the waffle is likely to break apart.

6

banana blueberry muffins

**2 ripe, medium DOLE®
Bananas**

**6 tablespoons
margarine**

**6 tablespoons brown
sugar**

1 egg

1½ cups all-purpose flour

**½ teaspoon baking
powder**

½ teaspoon baking soda

½ teaspoon salt

**½ teaspoon grated
lemon peel**

**1 cup frozen
blueberries, rinsed,
drained**

• Purée bananas in blender (1 cup).

• Beat margarine and sugar in large bowl until light and fluffy. Mix in bananas and egg.

• Combine flour, baking powder, baking soda, salt and lemon peel in medium bowl. Blend into margarine mixture just until moistened. Fold in blueberries.

• Line 6 large muffin cups with paper liners; spray lightly with vegetable cooking spray. Spoon batter evenly into cups.

• Bake at 375°F 20 to 25 minutes.   *makes 6 muffins*

prep time: 20 minutes
bake time: 25 minutes

super cinnamon bun

CINNAMON BUN

1 (16 ounce) package hot roll mix

1 cup QUAKER® Oats (quick or old fashioned, uncooked)

¾ cup raisins

½ cup sugar, divided

2½ teaspoons ground cinnamon, divided

1 cup hot water (120°F to 130°F)

1 egg, lightly beaten

5 tablespoons margarine or butter, melted, divided

GLAZE

¾ cup powdered sugar

3 to 4 teaspoons milk

½ teaspoon vanilla

Lightly grease large cookie sheet. In large bowl, combine hot roll mix, yeast packet, oats, raisins, ¼ cup sugar and 1½ teaspoons cinnamon. Stir in hot water, egg and 3 tablespoons melted margarine. Mix until dough pulls away from sides of bowl. Knead on lightly floured surface 5 minutes or until smooth and elastic. Divide into 4 equal pieces; roll each piece into 12-inch rope on lightly floured surface. In center of prepared cookie sheet, form a coil with one rope. Attach a second rope to the coiled rope by pressing the rope ends together firmly; continue coiling around the first rope. Repeat with the third and fourth ropes to form one large bun.

Combine remaining ¼ cup sugar, 1 teaspoon cinnamon and 2 tablespoons melted margarine. Brush evenly over top and sides of bun. Cover loosely with plastic wrap; let rise in warm place 30 minutes or until about double in size.

Heat oven to 375°F. Bake 30 to 35 minutes or until golden brown. Carefully remove to wire rack; cool slightly. For glaze, combine all ingredients; mix until smooth. Drizzle over bun. Serve warm or at room temperature. *makes 16 servings*

note: If the hot roll mix is not available, combine 3 cups all-purpose flour, 1 cup oats, ¾ cup raisins, two ¼-ounce packages quick-rising yeast, ⅓ cup granulated sugar, 1½ teaspoons salt and 1½ teaspoons cinnamon. Continue as recipe directs.

banana smoothies & pops

1 (14-ounce) can
   EAGLE® BRAND
   Sweetened
   Condensed Milk
   (NOT evaporated
   milk)
1 (8-ounce) container
   vanilla yogurt
2 ripe bananas
½ cup orange juice

Process Eagle Brand and remaining ingredients in blender until smooth, stopping to scrape down sides. Serve immediately.   *makes 4 cups*

banana smoothie pops: Spoon banana mixture into 8 (5-ounce) paper cups. Freeze 30 minutes. Insert wooden craft sticks into center of each cup; freeze until firm.

fruit smoothies: Substitute 1 cup of your favorite fruit and ½ cup any fruit juice for banana and orange juice.

prep time: 5 minutes

buttermilk pancakes

2 cups all-purpose flour
1 tablespoon sugar
1½ teaspoons baking
   powder
½ teaspoon baking soda
½ teaspoon salt
1 egg, beaten
1½ cups buttermilk
¼ cup vegetable oil

1. Sift flour, sugar, baking powder, baking soda and salt into large bowl.

2. Combine egg, buttermilk and oil in medium bowl. Stir liquid ingredients into dry ingredients until moistened.

3. Preheat griddle or large skillet over medium heat; grease lightly. Pour about ½ cup batter onto hot griddle for each pancake. Cook until tops of pancakes are bubbly and appear dry; turn and cook until browned, about 2 minutes.   *makes about 12 (5-inch) pancakes*

silver dollar pancakes: Use 1 tablespoon batter for each pancake. Cook as directed above.

buttermilk substitution: If you don't have buttermilk on hand, try this easy substitution. Place 1 tablespoon vinegar in measuring cup. Add milk to measure 1½ cups. Stir well; let stand 5 minutes.

chocolate quickie stickies

8 tablespoons (1 stick) butter or margarine, divided

¾ cup packed light brown sugar

4 tablespoons HERSHEY'S Cocoa, divided

5 teaspoons water

1 teaspoon vanilla extract

½ cup coarsely chopped nuts (optional)

2 cans (8 ounces each) refrigerated quick crescent dinner rolls

2 tablespoons granulated sugar

1. Heat oven to 350°F.

2. Melt 6 tablespoons butter in small saucepan over low heat; add brown sugar, 3 tablespoons cocoa and water. Cook over medium heat, stirring constantly, just until mixture comes to boil. Remove from heat; stir in vanilla. Spoon about 1 teaspoon chocolate mixture into each of 48 small muffin cups (1¾ inches in diameter). Sprinkle ½ teaspoon nuts, if desired, into each cup; set aside.

3. Unroll dough; separate into 8 rectangles; firmly press perforations to seal. Melt remaining 2 tablespoons butter; brush over rectangles. Stir together granulated sugar and remaining 1 tablespoon cocoa; sprinkle over rectangles. Starting at longer side, roll up each rectangle; pinch seams to seal. Cut each roll into 6 equal pieces. Press gently into prepared pans, cut-side down.

4. Bake 11 to 13 minutes or until light brown. Remove from oven; let cool 30 seconds. Invert onto cookie sheet. Let stand 1 minute; remove pans. Serve warm or cool completely.   *makes 4 dozen small rolls*

note: Rolls can be baked in two 8-inch round baking pans. Heat oven to 350°F. Cook chocolate mixture as directed; spread half of mixture in each pan. Prepare rolls as directed; place 24 pieces, cut-side down, in each pan. Bake 20 to 22 minutes. Cool and remove pans as directed above.

french toast sticks

1 cup EGG BEATERS®
Healthy Real Egg
Product

⅓ cup skim milk

1 teaspoon ground
cinnamon

1 teaspoon vanilla
extract

2 tablespoons
FLEISCHMANN'S®
Original Margarine,
divided

16 (4×1×1-inch) sticks
day-old white bread

Powdered sugar,
optional

Maple-flavored syrup,
optional

In shallow bowl, combine Egg Beaters®, milk, cinnamon and vanilla.

In large nonstick griddle or skillet, over medium-high heat, melt 2 teaspoons margarine. Dip bread sticks in egg mixture to coat; transfer to griddle. Cook sticks on each side until golden, adding remaining margarine as needed. Dust lightly with powdered sugar and serve with syrup, if desired.

makes 4 servings

prep time: 15 minutes
cook time: 18 minutes

fruit 'n juice breakfast shake

1 extra-ripe, medium
DOLE® Banana

¾ cup DOLE® Pineapple
Juice

½ cup low fat vanilla
yogurt

½ cup blueberries

Combine all ingredients in blender. Whir until smooth.

makes 2 servings

breakfast pizza

1 can (10 ounces) refrigerated biscuit dough

½ pound bacon slices

2 tablespoons butter or margarine

2 tablespoons all-purpose flour

¼ teaspoon salt

⅛ teaspoon black pepper

1½ cups milk

½ cup (2 ounces) shredded sharp Cheddar cheese

¼ cup sliced green onion

¼ cup chopped red bell pepper

Preheat oven to 350°F. Spray 13×9-inch baking dish with nonstick cooking spray.

Separate biscuit dough and arrange in rectangle on lightly floured surface. Roll into 14×10-inch rectangle. Place in prepared dish; pat edges up sides of dish. Bake 15 minutes. Remove from oven and set aside.

Meanwhile, place bacon in single layer in large skillet; cook over medium heat until crisp. Remove from skillet; drain on paper towels. Crumble and set aside.

Melt butter in medium saucepan over medium heat. Stir in flour, salt and black pepper until smooth. Gradually stir in milk; cook and stir until thickened. Stir in cheese until melted. Spread sauce evenly over baked crust. Arrange bacon, green onions and bell pepper over sauce.

Bake, uncovered, 20 minutes or until crust is golden brown.

makes 6 servings

Bacon can be cooked in the oven instead of in a skillet. Simply place bacon strips in a single layer on a baking sheet with sides and bake in a preheated 400°F oven for 10 to 15 minutes. Drain on paper towels before using.

bunny pancakes with strawberry butter

Strawberry Butter (recipe follows)

2 cups buttermilk baking mix

1 cup milk

2 eggs

½ cup plain yogurt

Assorted candies

1. Prepare Strawberry Butter; set aside. Preheat electric skillet or griddle to 375°F.

2. Combine baking mix, milk, eggs and yogurt in medium bowl; mix well. Spoon scant ½ cup batter into skillet. With back of spoon, gently spread batter into 4-inch circle. Spoon about 2 tablespoons batter onto top edge of circle for head. Using back of spoon, spread batter from head to form bunny ears as shown in photo.

3. Cook until bubbles on surface begin to pop and top of pancake appears dry; turn pancake over. Cook until done, 1 to 2 minutes. Decorate with candies as shown in photo.

4. Repeat with remaining batter. Serve warm with Strawberry Butter.

makes about 12 (8-inch) pancakes

strawberry butter: Place 1 package (3 ounces) softened cream cheese and ½ cup softened butter in food processor or blender; process until smooth. Add ⅓ cup powdered sugar; process until blended. Add 1½ cups fresh or thawed frozen strawberries; process until finely chopped.

cool 'n tropical treat

BREYERS® Lowfat Yogurt, any flavor

Low fat granola

COOL WHIP LITE® or FREE® Whipped Topping, thawed

Pineapple chunks, drained

ALTERNATE layers of yogurt, granola, whipped topping and pineapple chunks in glass or small bowl. Top with whipped topping.

makes 1 serving

best of the season: Use seasonal fresh berries in place of canned fruit, if desired.

prep time: 5 minutes

17

pb & j french toast

¼ cup preserves, any flavor

6 slices whole wheat bread, divided

¼ cup creamy peanut butter

½ cup egg substitute

¼ cup skim milk

2 tablespoons margarine or butter

1 large banana, sliced

1 tablespoon honey

1 tablespoon orange juice

1 tablespoon PLANTERS® Dry Roasted Unsalted Peanuts, chopped

Low fat vanilla yogurt, optional

1. Spread preserves evenly over 3 bread slices. Spread peanut butter evenly over remaining bread slices. Press preserves and peanut butter slices together to form 3 sandwiches; cut each diagonally in half.

2. Combine egg substitute and milk in shallow bowl. Dip each sandwich in egg mixture to coat.

3. Cook sandwiches in margarine or butter in large nonstick griddle or skillet over medium-high heat for 2 minutes on each side or until golden. Keep warm.

4. Mix banana slices, honey, orange juice and peanuts in small bowl. Arrange sandwiches on platter; top with banana mixture. Serve warm with a dollop of yogurt if desired. *makes 6 servings*

prep time: 25 minutes
cook time: 10 minutes

Bananas will ripen if they are kept uncovered at room temperature. To speed up the ripening process, place them in a perforated brown paper bag with a ripe apple.

18

fruit muffins

MUFFINS
- ⅔ cup milk
- 1 tablespoon oil
- 1 egg
- 2 cups packaged baking mix
- 2 tablespoons sugar
- ¼ cup SMUCKER'S® Preserves (any flavor)

GLAZE
- ⅔ cup powdered sugar
- 3 to 4 teaspoons milk

Grease bottom only of 12 medium muffin cups or line with paper baking cups. Combine milk, oil and egg; blend until well mixed. Add baking mix and sugar; stir just until moistened. Fill greased muffin cups ⅔ full. Drop 1 level teaspoon of preserves onto center of batter in each cup.

Bake at 400°F for 13 to 18 minutes or until golden brown. Cool slightly and remove from pan.

Stir together glaze ingredients until smooth, adding enough milk for desired glaze consistency. Drizzle over cooled muffins.

makes 12 muffins

ham & swiss cheese biscuits

- 2 cups all-purpose flour
- 2 teaspoons baking powder
- ½ teaspoon baking soda
- ½ cup butter, chilled and cut into pieces
- ½ cup (2 ounces) shredded Swiss cheese
- 2 ounces ham, minced
- About ⅔ cup buttermilk

1. Preheat oven to 450°F. Grease baking sheet.

2. Sift flour, baking powder and baking soda into medium bowl. Using pastry blender or 2 knives, cut in butter until mixture resembles coarse crumbs. Stir in cheese, ham and enough buttermilk to make soft dough.

3. Turn out dough onto lightly floured surface; knead lightly. Roll out dough ½ inch thick. Cut biscuit rounds with 2-inch cutter. Place on greased baking sheet.

4. Bake about 10 minutes or until browned.

makes about 18 biscuits

apple raisin pancakes

2 cups all-purpose flour

2 tablespoons sugar

1 tablespoon baking powder

2 teaspoons ground cinnamon

1¾ cups fat-free (skim) milk

⅔ cup EGG BEATERS® Healthy Real Egg Product

5 tablespoons FLEISCHMANN'S® Original Margarine, melted, divided

¾ cup chopped apple

¾ cup seedless raisins

In large bowl, combine flour, sugar, baking powder and cinnamon. In medium bowl, combine milk, Egg Beaters® and 4 tablespoons margarine; stir into dry ingredients just until blended. Stir in apple and raisins.

Brush large nonstick griddle or skillet with some of remaining margarine; heat over medium-high heat. Using ¼ cup batter for each pancake, pour batter onto griddle. Cook until bubbly; turn and cook until lightly browned. Repeat with remaining batter using remaining margarine as needed to make 16 pancakes.

makes 16 (4-inch) pancakes

prep time: 10 minutes
cook time: 15 minutes

BREAKFAST

streusel coffeecake

32 CHIPS AHOY!®
   Chocolate Chip
   Cookies, divided
1 (18- to 18.5-ounce)
   package yellow or
   white cake mix
½ cup sour cream
½ cup PLANTERS®
   Pecans, chopped
½ cup flaked coconut
¼ cup packed brown
   sugar
1 teaspoon ground
   cinnamon
⅓ cup margarine or
   butter, melted
   Powdered sugar glaze,
   optional

1. Coarsely chop 20 cookies; finely crush remaining 12 cookies. Set aside.

2. Prepare cake mix batter according to package directions; blend in sour cream. Stir in chopped cookies. Pour batter into greased and floured 13×9×2-inch baking pan.

3. Mix cookie crumbs, pecans, coconut, brown sugar and cinnamon; stir in margarine or butter. Sprinkle over cake batter.

4. Bake at 350°F for 40 minutes or until toothpick inserted in center of cake comes out clean. Cool completely. Drizzle with powdered sugar glaze if desired. Cut into squares to serve.   *makes 24 servings*

preparation time: 25 minutes
cook time: 40 minutes
cooling time: 2 hours
total time: 3 hours and 5 minutes

spiced apple toast.

1 tablespoon margarine
2 all-purpose apples,
   unpeeled, cored and
   thinly sliced
⅓ cup orange juice
4 teaspoons packed
   brown sugar
½ teaspoon ground
   cinnamon
4 slices whole wheat
   bread, toasted
2 teaspoons granulated
   sugar

Preheat oven to 450°F. Melt margarine in medium nonstick skillet. Add apples, orange juice, brown sugar and cinnamon; cook over medium-high heat about 4 minutes or until apples are tender, stirring occasionally. Drain; reserve cooking liquid. Cool apples 2 to 3 minutes. Place toast on lightly buttered baking sheet. Arrange apples, overlapping slices, in spiral design. Sprinkle ½ teaspoon granulated sugar over each slice. Bake 4 to 5 minutes or until bread is crisp. Drizzle reserved liquid over slices; serve immediately.

makes 4 servings

Favorite recipe from **The Sugar Association, Inc.**

22

streusel coffeecake

chocolate chip waffles

1 package DUNCAN HINES® Chocolate Chip Muffin Mix

¾ cup all-purpose flour

1 teaspoon baking powder

1¾ cups milk

2 eggs

5 tablespoons butter or margarine, melted

Confectioners' sugar (optional)

Preheat and lightly grease waffle iron according to manufacturer's directions.

Combine muffin mix, flour and baking powder in large bowl. Add milk, eggs and melted butter. Stir until moistened, about 50 strokes. Pour batter onto center grids of preheated waffle iron. Bake according to manufacturer's directions until golden brown. Remove baked waffle carefully with fork. Repeat with remaining batter. Dust lightly with sugar, if desired. Top with fresh fruit, syrup, grated chocolate or whipped cream, if desired.   *makes 10 to 12 waffles*

banana chocolate chip muffins

2 ripe, medium DOLE® Bananas

2 eggs

1 cup packed brown sugar

½ cup margarine, melted

1 teaspoon vanilla extract

2¼ cups all-purpose flour

2 teaspoons baking powder

½ teaspoon ground cinnamon

½ teaspoon salt

1 cup chocolate chips

½ cup chopped walnuts

• Purée bananas in blender (1 cup). Beat bananas, eggs, sugar, margarine and vanilla in medium bowl until well blended.

• Combine flour, baking powder, cinnamon and salt in large bowl. Stir in chocolate chips and nuts. Make well in center of dry ingredients. Add banana mixture. Stir just until blended. Spoon into well greased 2½-inch muffin pan cups.

• Bake at 350°F, 25 to 30 minutes or until toothpick inserted in center comes out clean. Cool slightly, remove from pan and place on wire rack.
                makes 12 muffins

prep time: 20 minutes
bake time: 30 minutes

24

apple & raisin oven pancake

1 large baking apple,
cored and thinly
sliced

⅓ cup golden raisins

2 tablespoons packed
brown sugar

½ teaspoon ground
cinnamon

4 eggs

⅔ cup milk

⅔ cup all-purpose flour

2 tablespoons butter or
margarine, melted

Powdered sugar
(optional)

Preheat oven to 350°F. Spray 9-inch pie plate with nonstick cooking spray.

Combine apple, raisins, brown sugar and cinnamon in medium bowl. Transfer to prepared pie plate.

Bake, uncovered, 10 to 15 minutes or until apple begins to soften. Remove from oven. *Increase oven temperature to 450°F.*

Meanwhile, whisk eggs, milk, flour and butter in medium bowl until blended. Pour batter over apple mixture.

Bake 15 minutes or until pancake is golden brown. Invert onto serving dish. Sprinkle with powdered sugar, if desired.   *makes 6 servings*

maple apple oatmeal

2 cups apple juice

1½ cups water

⅓ cup AUNT JEMIMA®
Syrup

½ teaspoon ground
cinnamon

¼ teaspoon salt
(optional)

2 cups QUAKER® Oats
(quick or old
fashioned,
uncooked)

1 cup chopped fresh
unpeeled apple
(about 1 medium)

In 3-quart saucepan, bring juice, water, syrup, cinnamon and salt to a boil. Stir in oats and apple. Return to a boil; reduce heat to medium-low. Cook about 1 minute for quick oats (or 5 minutes for old fashioned oats) or until most of liquid is absorbed, stirring occasionally. Let stand until of desired consistency.   *makes 4 servings*

orange cinnamon swirl bread

BREAD

1 package DUNCAN HINES® Cinnamon Swirl Muffin Mix

1 egg

⅔ cup orange juice

1 tablespoon grated orange peel

ORANGE GLAZE

½ cup confectioners' sugar

2 to 3 teaspoons orange juice

1 teaspoon grated orange peel

Quartered orange slices, for garnish (optional)

1. Preheat oven to 350°F. Grease and flour 8½×4½×2½-inch loaf pan.

2. For bread, combine muffin mix and contents of topping packet from mix in large bowl. Break up any lumps. Add egg, ⅔ cup orange juice and 1 tablespoon orange peel. Stir until moistened, about 50 strokes. Knead swirl packet from mix for 10 seconds before opening. Squeeze contents on top of batter. Swirl into batter with knife or spatula, folding from bottom of bowl to get an even swirl. *Do not completely mix in.* Pour into pan. Bake at 350°F 55 to 60 minutes or until toothpick inserted in center comes out clean. Cool in pan 10 minutes. Loosen loaf from pan. Invert onto cooling rack. Turn right side up. Cool completely.

3. For orange glaze, place confectioners' sugar in small bowl. Add orange juice, 1 teaspoon at a time, stirring until smooth and desired consistency. Stir in 1 teaspoon orange peel. Drizzle over loaf. Garnish with orange slices, if desired.   *makes 1 loaf (12 slices)*

tip: If glaze becomes too thin, add more confectioners' sugar. If glaze is too thick, add more orange juice.

creamy cinnamon rolls

2 (1-pound) loaves
    frozen bread dough,
    thawed

⅔ cup (one-half
    14-ounce can)
    EAGLE® BRAND
    Sweetened
    Condensed Milk
    (NOT evaporated
    milk), divided*

1 cup chopped pecans

2 teaspoons ground
    cinnamon

1 cup sifted powdered
    sugar

½ teaspoon vanilla
    extract

Additional chopped
    pecans (optional)

Use remaining Eagle Brand as a dip for fruit. Pour into storage container and store tightly covered in refrigerator for up to 1 week.

1. On lightly floured surface roll each of bread dough loaves to 12×9-inch rectangle. Spread ⅓ cup Eagle Brand over dough rectangles. Sprinkle with 1 cup pecans and cinnamon. Roll up jelly-roll style starting from a short side. Cut each into 6 slices.

2. Generously grease 13×9-inch baking pan. Place rolls cut sides down in pan. Cover loosely with greased waxed paper and then with plastic wrap. Chill overnight. Cover and chill remaining Eagle Brand.

3. To bake, let pan of rolls stand at room temperature for 30 minutes. Preheat oven to 350°F. Bake 30 to 35 minutes or until golden brown. Cool in pan 5 minutes; loosen edges and remove rolls from pan.

4. Meanwhile for frosting, in small bowl, combine powdered sugar, remaining ⅓ cup Eagle Brand and vanilla. Drizzle frosting on warm rolls. Sprinkle with additional chopped pecans. *makes 12 rolls*

prep time: 20 minutes
bake time: 30 to 35 minutes
chill time: overnight
cool time: 5 minutes

tooty fruitys

1 package (10 ounces)
  extra-light flaky
  biscuits
10 (1½-inch) fruit pieces
1 egg white
1 teaspoon water
Powdered sugar
  (optional)

1. Preheat oven to 425°F. Spray baking sheets with nonstick cooking spray; set aside.

2. Separate biscuits. Place on lightly floured surface. Roll with lightly floured rolling pin or flatten dough with fingers to form 3½-inch circles. Place 1 fruit piece in center of each circle. Bring 3 edges of dough up over fruit; pinch edges together to seal. Place on prepared baking sheet.

3. Beat egg white with water in small bowl; brush over dough.

4. Bake until golden brown, 10 to 15 minutes. Remove to wire rack to cool. Serve warm or at room temperature. Sprinkle with powdered sugar just before serving. *makes 10 servings*

sweet tooty fruitys: Prepare dough circles as directed. Gently press both sides of dough circles into granulated or cinnamon-sugar to coat completely. Top with fruit and continue as directed, except do not brush with egg white mixture or sprinkle with powdered sugar.

cheesy tooty fruitys: Prepare dough circles as directed. Top each circle with ½ teaspoon softened reduced-fat cream cheese in addition to the fruit. Continue as directed.

sugar and cinnamon apple muffins

MUFFINS

1 egg

⅔ cup apple juice or milk

½ cup oil

1 teaspoon vanilla

2 cups all-purpose flour

¼ cup DOMINO® Granulated Sugar

¼ cup firmly packed DOMINO® Light Brown Sugar

1 tablespoon baking powder

½ teaspoon salt

1½ cups cored and chopped apple

½ cup chopped nuts

TOPPING

2 tablespoons DOMINO® Granulated Sugar

1 teaspoon cinnamon

Heat oven to 400°F. Grease bottoms of 12 medium muffin cups or line with paper baking cups.

Beat egg with juice, oil and vanilla in medium bowl. Stir in flour, sugars, baking powder and salt just until flour is moistened (batter will be lumpy). Stir in apple and nuts. Fill muffin cups.

Combine topping ingredients in small bowl; sprinkle over batter in muffin cups.

Bake at 400°F. for 20 to 22 minutes or until golden brown. Immediately remove from pan to cooling rack. *makes 12 muffins*

preparation time: 20 minutes
bake time: 22 minutes

Don't stir muffin batter too vigorously or you'll end up with tough muffins. Just stir until all the dry ingredients are moistened; any lumps will disappear during baking.

cinnamon fruit crunch

1 cup low-fat granola cereal

¼ cup toasted sliced almonds

1 tablespoon margarine

2 tablespoons plus 1 teaspoon packed brown sugar, divided

2¼ teaspoons ground cinnamon, divided

½ cup vanilla yogurt

⅛ teaspoon ground nutmeg

2 cans (16 ounces each) mixed fruit chunks in juice, drained

Combine granola and almonds in small bowl. Melt margarine in small saucepan. Blend in 2 tablespoons brown sugar and 2 teaspoons cinnamon; simmer until sugar dissolves, about 2 minutes. Toss with granola and almonds; cool. Combine yogurt, remaining 1 teaspoon brown sugar, ¼ teaspoon cinnamon and nutmeg in small bowl. To serve, spoon approximately ½ cup chunky mixed fruit onto each serving plate. Top with yogurt mixture and sprinkle with granola mixture.

makes 6 servings

peanut butter & banana wake-up shake

1 cup (8 ounces) vanilla yogurt

1 cup milk

⅓ cup SKIPPY® Creamy Peanut Butter

¼ cup KARO® Light or Dark Corn Syrup

1 ripe banana, cut in chunks

5 ice cubes

1. In blender combine yogurt, milk, peanut butter, corn syrup and banana; blend until smooth.

2. With blender running, gradually add ice cubes. Blend until thickened and smooth. Serve immediately. *makes about 4 (8-ounce) servings*

prep time: 5 minutes

orange smoothies

1 cup fat-free vanilla ice
cream or fat-free
vanilla frozen yogurt

¾ cup low-fat (1%) milk

¼ cup frozen orange
juice concentrate

1. Combine ice cream, milk and orange juice concentrate in food processor or blender; process until smooth.

2. Pour mixture into 2 glasses; garnish as desired. Serve immediately.

makes 2 servings

chocolate quicky sticky bread

2 loaves (16 ounces
each) frozen bread
dough

¾ cup granulated sugar

1 tablespoon
HERSHEY'S Cocoa

1 teaspoon ground
cinnamon

½ cup (1 stick) butter or
margarine, melted
and divided

½ cup packed light
brown sugar

¼ cup water

HERSHEY'S MINI
KISSES™ Semi-
Sweet or Milk
Chocolate Baking
Pieces

1. Thaw loaves as directed on package; let rise until doubled.

2. Stir together granulated sugar, cocoa and cinnamon. In small microwave-safe bowl, stir together ¼ cup butter, brown sugar and water. Microwave at HIGH (100%) 30 to 60 seconds or until smooth when stirred. Pour mixture into 12-cup fluted tube pan.

3. Heat oven to 350°F. Pinch off pieces of bread dough; form into balls, 1½ inches in diameter, placing 3 Mini Kisses™ inside each ball. Dip each ball in remaining ¼ cup butter; roll in cocoa-sugar mixture. Place balls in prepared pan.

4. Bake 45 to 50 minutes or until golden brown. Cool 20 minutes in pan; invert onto serving plate. Cool until lukewarm.

makes 12 servings

peanut butter mini muffins

⅓ cup creamy peanut butter

¼ cup (½ stick) butter, softened

¼ cup granulated sugar

¼ cup firmly packed light brown sugar

1 large egg

¾ cup buttermilk

3 tablespoons vegetable oil

¾ teaspoon vanilla extract

1½ cups all-purpose flour

¾ teaspoon baking powder

½ teaspoon baking soda

½ teaspoon salt

1¼ cups "M&M's"® Milk Chocolate Mini Baking Bits, divided

Chocolate Glaze (recipe follows)

Preheat oven to 350°F. Lightly grease 36 (1¾-inch) mini muffin cups or line with paper or foil liners; set aside. In large bowl cream peanut butter, butter and sugars until light and fluffy; beat in egg. Beat in buttermilk, oil and vanilla. In medium bowl combine flour, baking powder, baking soda and salt; gradually blend into creamed mixture. Divide batter evenly among prepared muffin cups. Sprinkle batter evenly with ¾ cup "M&M's"® Milk Chocolate Mini Baking Bits. Bake 15 to 17 minutes or until toothpick inserted in centers comes out clean. Cool completely on wire racks. Prepare Chocolate Glaze. Place glaze in resealable plastic sandwich bag; seal bag. Cut tiny piece off one corner of bag (not more than ⅛ inch). Drizzle glaze over muffins. Decorate with remaining ½ cup "M&M's"® Milk Chocolate Mini Baking Bits. Store in tightly covered container.   *makes 3 dozen mini muffins*

chocolate glaze: In top of double boiler over hot water, melt 2 (1-ounce) squares semi-sweet chocolate and 1 tablespoon butter. Stir until smooth; let cool slightly.

36

cereal trail mix

¼ cup butter or margarine

2 tablespoons sugar

1 teaspoon ground cinnamon

1 cup bite-sized oat cereal squares

1 cup bite-sized wheat cereal squares

1 cup bite-sized rice cereal squares

¼ cup toasted slivered almonds

¾ cup raisins

1. Melt butter at HIGH (100%) 1½ minutes in large microwave-safe bowl. Add sugar and cinnamon; mix well. Add cereals and nuts; stir to coat.

2. Microwave at HIGH 2 minutes. Stir well. Microwave 2 minutes more; stir well. Add raisins. Microwave an additional 2 to 3 minutes, stirring well after 2 minutes. Spread on paper towels; mix will become crisp as it cools. Store tightly covered.   *makes about 4 cups*

breakfast blossoms

1 (12-ounce) can buttermilk biscuits (10 biscuits)

¾ cup SMUCKER'S® Strawberry Preserves

¼ teaspoon ground cinnamon

¼ teaspoon ground nutmeg

Grease ten 2½- or 3-inch muffin cups. Separate dough into 10 biscuits. Separate each biscuit into 3 even sections or leaves. Stand 3 sections evenly around sides and bottom of cup, overlapping slightly. Press dough edges firmly together.

Combine preserves, cinnamon and nutmeg; place scant tablespoonful in center of each cup.

Bake at 375°F for 10 to 12 minutes or until lightly browned. Cool slightly before removing from pan. Serve warm.   *makes 10 rolls*

strawberry muffins

1¼ cups all-purpose flour

2½ teaspoons baking powder

½ teaspoon salt

1 cup uncooked old-fashioned oats

½ cup sugar

1 cup milk

½ cup butter, melted

1 egg, beaten

1 teaspoon vanilla

1 cup chopped fresh strawberries

Preheat oven to 425°F. Grease 12 (2½-inch) muffin cups; set aside.

Combine flour, baking powder and salt in large bowl. Stir in oats and sugar. Combine milk, butter, egg and vanilla in small bowl until well blended; stir into flour mixture just until moistened. Fold in strawberries. Spoon into prepared muffin cups, filling about two-thirds full.

Bake 15 to 18 minutes or until lightly browned and toothpick inserted in center comes out clean. Remove from pan. Cool on wire rack 10 minutes. Serve warm or cool completely.   *makes 12 muffins*

pumpkin bread

1 package (about 18 ounces) yellow cake mix

⅓ cup GRANDMA'S® Molasses (gold label)

4 eggs

1 can (16 ounces) solid pack pumpkin

1 teaspoon cinnamon

1 teaspoon nutmeg

⅓ cup nuts, chopped (optional)

⅓ cup raisins (optional)

Preheat oven to 350°F. Grease two 9×5-inch loaf pans.

Combine all ingredients in a large bowl and mix well. Beat at medium speed 2 minutes. Pour into prepared pans. Bake 60 minutes or until toothpick inserted in center comes out clean.   *makes 2 loaves*

hint: Serve with cream cheese or preserves, or top with cream cheese frosting or ice cream.

apple cinnamon quesadillas

Spiced Yogurt Dipping Sauce (recipe follows)

1 medium McIntosh apple, cored and chopped

¾ cup no-sugar-added applesauce

⅛ teaspoon ground cinnamon

4 flour tortillas (6-inch)

¼ cup (1 ounce) shredded reduced-fat Cheddar cheese

Nonstick cooking spray

1. Prepare Spiced Yogurt Dipping Sauce. Set aside.

2. Combine apple, applesauce and cinnamon in small bowl; mix well.

3. Spoon half of apple mixture onto tortilla; sprinkle with half of cheese. Top with another tortilla. Repeat with remaining tortillas and apple mixture.

4. Spray large nonstick skillet with cooking spray; heat over medium heat until hot. Cook quesadillas, one at a time, about 2 minutes on each side or until golden brown. Cut each quesadilla into four wedges. Serve with Spiced Yogurt Dipping Sauce. *makes 4 servings*

spiced yogurt dipping sauce

½ cup vanilla low-fat yogurt

2 tablespoons no-sugar-added applesauce

Dash ground cinnamon

Combine yogurt, applesauce and cinnamon in small bowl; mix well. Refrigerate until ready to use.

ham and cheese corn muffins

1 package (8½ ounces)
    corn muffin mix
½ cup chopped deli ham
½ cup (2 ounces)
    shredded Swiss
    cheese
⅓ cup reduced-fat (2%)
    milk
1 egg
1 tablespoon Dijon
    mustard

1. Preheat oven to 400°F. Combine muffin mix, ham and cheese in medium bowl.

2. Combine milk, egg and mustard in 1-cup glass measure. Stir milk mixture into dry ingredients; mix just until moistened.

3. Fill 9 paper cup-lined 2¾-inch muffin cups two-thirds full with batter.

4. Bake 18 to 20 minutes or until light golden brown. Remove muffin pan to cooling rack. Let stand 5 minutes. Serve warm.

makes 9 muffins

serving suggestion: For added flavor, serve Ham and Cheese Corn Muffins with honey-flavored butter. To prepare, stir together equal amounts of honey and softened butter.

prep and cook time: 30 minutes

hearty banana carrot muffins

2 ripe, medium DOLE®
    Bananas
1 package (14 ounces)
    oat bran muffin mix
¾ teaspoon ground
    ginger
1 medium DOLE®
    Carrot, shredded
    (½ cup)
⅓ cup light molasses
⅓ cup DOLE® Raisins
¼ cup chopped almonds

• Mash bananas with fork. (1 cup)

• Combine muffin mix and ginger in large bowl. Add carrot, molasses, raisins and bananas. Stir just until moistened.

• Spoon batter into paper-lined muffin cups. Sprinkle tops with almonds.

• Bake at 425°F 12 to 14 minutes until browned.   *makes 12 muffins*

prep time: 20 minutes
bake time: 14 minutes

43

crispy's™ vanishing pancakes

2 cups all-purpose flour

1 tablespoon granulated sugar

1½ teaspoons baking powder

½ teaspoon baking soda

½ teaspoon salt

1 large egg

1½ cups buttermilk

¼ cup vegetable oil

¾ cup "M&M's"® Semi-Sweet Chocolate Mini Baking Bits, divided

Butter and maple syrup

Lightly grease and preheat griddle or large skillet over medium heat. In large bowl combine flour, sugar, baking powder, baking soda and salt. In medium bowl beat egg; gradually add buttermilk and oil until well blended. Blend egg mixture into flour mixture just until moistened. For each pancake, pour about ½ cup batter onto hot griddle. Sprinkle with about 1 tablespoon "M&M's"® Semi-Sweet Chocolate Mini Baking Bits. Cook until tops of pancakes appear dry; turn with spatula and cook 2 minutes or until golden brown. Serve with butter, maple syrup and remaining ¼ cup "M&M's"® Semi-Sweet Chocolate Mini Baking Bits.

makes 6 to 8 (5-inch) pancakes

cool yogurt smoothie

1 container (8 ounces) BREYERS® Strawberry Lowfat Yogurt, any variety

½ tub (8 ounces) COOL WHIP® Whipped Topping, thawed or frozen

1 cup fresh or frozen strawberries or any other seasonal fruit, chopped (optional)

PLACE yogurt, whipped topping and fruit in blender container; cover. Blend until smooth. (For thinner consistency, add ice cubes.) Serve immediately.

makes 2 servings

storage know-how: Smoothie can be covered and stored in the refrigerator up to 24 hours, or frozen up to 1 week. Reblend before serving. (Thaw frozen smoothie 20 minutes before blending.)

prep time: 1 minute

french raisin toast

2 tablespoons granulated sugar

1 teaspoon ground cinnamon

4 eggs, lightly beaten

½ cup milk

8 slices raisin bread

4 tablespoons butter or margarine, divided

Powdered sugar

1. Combine granulated sugar and cinnamon in wide shallow bowl. Beat in eggs and milk. Add bread; let stand to coat, then turn to coat other side.

2. Heat 2 tablespoons butter in large skillet over medium-low heat. Add 4 bread slices; cook until brown. Turn and cook other side. Remove; keep warm. Repeat with remaining butter and bread. Sprinkle with powdered sugar. Garnish as desired. Serve immediately.

makes 4 servings

note: Freezer burn, which is indicated by dry white or gray patches on the surface of frozen foods, is caused by improper wrapping. Food that is freezer burned is safe to eat. Just trim off the affected areas because they have an unpleasant flavor.

tunnel of cheese muffins

2 cups biscuit mix

5 slices bacon, crisply cooked and crumbled

¾ cup milk

1 egg, beaten

12 (½-inch) cubes Swiss cheese

Stir together biscuit mix and bacon in medium bowl. Add milk and egg, stirring just to mix. Spoon half of batter into 12 buttered muffin pan cups. Press one cheese cube in each cup. Top with remaining batter, covering cheese completely. Bake in preheated 400°F oven 25 minutes or until golden. Serve hot. *makes 12 muffins*

Favorite recipe from **Wisconsin Milk Marketing Board**

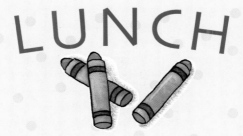

LUNCH

funny face sandwich melts

2 super-size English muffins, split and toasted

8 teaspoons *French's®* Honey Mustard

1 can (8 ounces) crushed pineapple, drained

8 ounces sliced smoked ham

4 slices Swiss cheese or white American cheese

1. Place English muffins, cut side up, on baking sheet. Spread each with *2 teaspoons* mustard. Arrange one-fourth of the pineapple, ham and cheese on top, dividing evenly.

2. Broil until cheese melts, about 1 minute. Decorate with mustard and assorted vegetables to create your own funny face.   *makes 4 servings*

tip: This sandwich is also easy to prepare in the toaster oven.

prep time: 10 minutes
cook time: 1 minute

peanut pitas

1 package (8 ounces)
small pita breads,
cut crosswise in half

16 teaspoons reduced-fat
peanut butter

16 teaspoons strawberry
spreadable fruit

1 large banana, peeled
and thinly sliced
(about 48 slices)

1. Spread inside of each pita half with 1 teaspoon each peanut butter and spreadable fruit.

2. Fill pita halves evenly with banana slices. Serve immediately.

makes 8 servings

honey bees: Substitute honey for spreadable fruit.

jolly jellies: Substitute any flavor jelly for spreadable fruit and thin apple slices for banana slices.

p. b. crunchers: Substitute reduced fat mayonnaise for spreadable fruit and celery slices for banana slices.

fiesta chicken soup

6 TYSON® Individually
Fresh Frozen®
Boneless, Skinless
Chicken Tenderloins

½ cup UNCLE BEN'S®
Instant Rice

2 cans (14½ ounces
each) low-sodium
chicken broth

1 can (15 ounces)
kidney beans,
undrained

1 cup salsa

1 cup frozen whole-
kernel corn

⅓ cup shredded
Monterey Jack
cheese

PREP: CLEAN: Wash hands. Remove protective ice glaze from frozen chicken by holding under cool running water 1 to 2 minutes. Cut chicken into 1-inch pieces. CLEAN: Wash hands.

COOK: In large saucepan, combine chicken, chicken broth, kidney beans, salsa and corn. Bring to a boil. Reduce heat and simmer, uncovered, 5 to 10 minutes or until internal juices of chicken run clear. (Or insert instant-read meat thermometer in thickest part of chicken. Temperature should read 170°F.) Stir in rice, cover and remove from heat. Let stand 5 minutes.

SERVE: Top individual servings of soup with cheese. Serve with fresh fruit and cornbread, if desired.

CHILL: Refrigerate leftovers immediately.

makes 4 servings

prep time: 10 minutes
cook time: 20 minutes

double-sauced chicken pizza bagels

1 whole bagel, split in half

4 tablespoons prepared pizza sauce

½ cup diced cooked chicken breast

¼ cup (1 ounce) shredded part-skim mozzarella cheese

2 teaspoons grated Parmesan cheese

1. Place bagel halves on microwavable plate.

2. Spoon 1 tablespoon pizza sauce onto each bagel half. Spread evenly using back of spoon.

3. Top each bagel half with ¼ cup chicken. Spoon 1 tablespoon pizza sauce over chicken on each bagel half.

4. Sprinkle 2 tablespoons mozzarella cheese over top of each bagel half.

5. Cover bagel halves loosely with waxed paper and microwave at HIGH 1 to 1½ minutes or until cheese melts.

6. Carefully remove waxed paper. Sprinkle each bagel half with 1 teaspoon Parmesan cheese. Let stand 1 minute before eating to cool slightly. (Bagels will be very hot.)

makes 2 servings (1 bagel half each)

tip: For crunchier "pizzas," toast bagels before adding toppings.

double-sauced chicken pizza bagel

chunky potato bacon soup

- 1 package (32 ounces) frozen Southern-style hash brown potatoes, thawed
- 1 quart milk
- 1 can (10¾ ounces) condensed cream of celery soup
- 1 cup (6 ounces) cubed processed cheese
- ⅓ cup cooked chopped bacon (4 slices uncooked)
- 1 tablespoon *French's®* Worcestershire Sauce
- 1⅓ cups *French's® Taste Toppers™* French Fried Onions

1. Combine potatoes, milk, soup, cheese, bacon and Worcestershire in large saucepot. Heat to boiling over medium-high heat, stirring often.

2. Heat *Taste Toppers* in microwave on HIGH 2 minutes or until golden. Ladle soup into bowls. Sprinkle with *Taste Toppers*. Garnish with fresh minced parsley if desired. *makes 6 servings*

prep time: 5 minutes
cook time: 10 minutes

Make soup more exciting by serving it in an edible bowl, such as a French roll or small round sourdough loaf. Simply slice a small piece from the top of the bread, then remove the center, leaving a 1-inch shell. Toast the bread bowls lightly before filling them with soup. These bowls are great for thicker soups and stews (such as chowders or chili), but they cannot be used to hold thin soups (such as chicken noodle).

crunchy turkey pita pockets

1 cup diced cooked turkey or chicken breast or reduced-sodium deli turkey breast

½ cup packaged cole slaw mix

½ cup dried cranberries

¼ cup shredded carrots

2 tablespoons reduced-fat or fat-free mayonnaise

1 tablespoon honey mustard

2 whole wheat pita breads

1. Combine turkey, cole slaw mix, cranberries, carrots, mayonnaise and mustard in small bowl; mix well.

2. Cut pita breads in half; fill with turkey mixture.

makes 2 servings

tuna sandwich melts

1 can (6 ounces) tuna in water, drained, flaked

½ cup MIRACLE WHIP® Salad Dressing

¼ pound (4 ounces) VELVEETA® Pasteurized Prepared Cheese Product, cut up

½ cup sliced celery

¼ cup chopped onion

4 Kaiser rolls, split

1. Mix all ingredients except rolls.

2. Fill each roll with ⅓ cup tuna mixture; wrap in foil.

3. Bake at 375°F for 20 to 25 minutes or until thoroughly heated.

makes 4 sandwiches

use your microwave: Prepare sandwiches as directed except for wrapping in foil. Place 2 sandwiches on paper towel. Microwave on HIGH 1 minute or until thoroughly heated. Repeat with remaining sandwiches.

prep time: 15 minutes
bake time: 25 minutes

kids' wrap

4 teaspoons Dijon honey mustard

2 (8-inch) fat-free flour tortillas

2 slices reduced-fat American cheese, torn into halves

4 ounces fat-free oven-roasted turkey breast

½ cup shredded carrots (about 1 medium)

3 romaine lettuce leaves, washed and torn into bite-size pieces

1. Spread 2 teaspoons mustard evenly over one tortilla.

2. Top with 2 cheese halves, half of turkey, half of shredded carrots and half of torn lettuce.

3. Roll up tortilla and cut in half. Repeat with remaining ingredients.

makes 2 servings

super spread sandwich stars

1 Red or Golden Delicious apple, peeled, cored and coarsely chopped

1 cup roasted peanuts

⅓ cup honey

1 tablespoon lemon juice

1 teaspoon ground cinnamon

Sliced sandwich bread

For Super Spread, place chopped apple, peanuts, honey, lemon juice and cinnamon in food processor or blender. Pulse food processor several times until ingredients start to blend, occasionally scraping down the sides with rubber spatula. Process 1 to 2 minutes until mixture is smooth and spreadable.

For Sandwich Stars, use butter knife to spread about 1 tablespoon Super Spread on 2 slices of bread. Stack them together, spread side up. Top with third slice bread. Place cookie cutter on top of sandwich; press down firmly and evenly. Leaving cookie cutter in place, remove excess trimmings with your fingers or a butter knife. Remove cookie cutter. *makes 1¼ cups spread (enough for about 10 sandwiches)*

Favorite recipe from **Texas Peanut Producers Board**

54

bologna "happy faces"

4 slices whole wheat or rye bread

1 cup prepared oil and vinegar based coleslaw

8 ounces HEBREW NATIONAL® Sliced Lean Beef Bologna or Lean Beef Salami

4 large pimiento-stuffed green olives

HEBREW NATIONAL® Deli Mustard

For each sandwich, spread 1 bread slice with 3 tablespoons coleslaw; top with 5 slices bologna. Cut olives in half crosswise; place over bologna for "eyes." Draw smiley "mouth" with mustard. Drop 1 tablespoon coleslaw at top of face for "hair."

makes 4 open-faced sandwiches

cheesy baked potato soup

¾ cup chopped onion

2 tablespoons butter or margarine

2 cups water

1 can (14½ ounces) chicken broth

2 to 3 large baked potatoes, cubed

Dash pepper

¾ pound (12 ounces) VELVEETA® Pasteurized Prepared Cheese Product, cut up

1. Cook and stir onion in butter in large saucepan on medium-high heat until tender.

2. Stir in water, broth, potatoes and pepper; heat thoroughly.

3. Add Velveeta; stir on low heat until melted. Serve with bacon bits, BREAKSTONE'S® or KNUDSEN® Sour Cream and chopped fresh parsley, if desired.

makes 6 cups

prep time: 15 minutes plus baking potatoes
cook time: 15 minutes

56

pizza rollers

1 package (10 ounces) refrigerated pizza dough
½ cup pizza sauce
18 slices turkey pepperoni
6 sticks mozzarella cheese

1. Preheat oven to 425°F. Coat baking sheet with nonstick cooking spray.

2. Roll out pizza dough on baking sheet to form 12×9-inch rectangle. Cut pizza dough into 6 (4½×4-inch) rectangles. Spread about 1 tablespoon sauce over center third of each rectangle. Top with 3 slices pepperoni and stick of mozzarella cheese. Bring ends of dough together over cheese, pinching to seal. Place, seam side down, on prepared baking sheet.

3. Bake in center of oven 10 minutes or until golden brown.

makes 6 servings

lunch box handwiches

1 package BOB EVANS® Frozen White Dinner Roll Dough
1 pound BOB EVANS® Italian Roll Sausage
⅓ cup tomato sauce
½ cup (2 ounces) shredded mozzarella or Cheddar cheese
1 egg yolk
1 tablespoon water

Thaw dough at room temperature 45 minutes to 1 hour. Allow dough to rise according to package directions. Preheat oven to 375°F. Crumble and cook sausage in medium skillet until browned. Drain off any drippings; let cool. Punch down dough; press each piece into 5- to 6-inch circle. Place about ⅓ cup cooked sausage, 2 teaspoons sauce and 1 tablespoon cheese on each circle; press filling down to flatten. Bring edges up over filling and seal edges to form a ball. Place seam sides down on greased baking sheet. Beat egg yolk and water; brush tops of dough with mixture. Bake 15 to 20 minutes or until golden brown. Serve warm, or cool, wrap and freeze to reheat and serve another time. Refrigerate leftovers. *makes 7 handwiches*

serving suggestion: Serve handwiches with a dipping sauce, such as tomato, pizza or spaghetti sauce.

chicken nuggets with barbecue dipping sauce

1 pound boneless
   skinless chicken
   breasts

¼ cup all-purpose flour

¼ teaspoon salt
   (optional)

   Black pepper to taste

2 cups crushed
   reduced-fat baked
   cheese crackers

1 teaspoon dried
   oregano leaves

1 egg white

1 tablespoon water

3 tablespoons barbecue
   sauce

2 tablespoons no-sugar-
   added peach or
   apricot jam

1. Preheat oven to 400°F. Rinse chicken. Pat dry with paper towels. Cut into 1-inch chunks.

2. Place flour, salt and pepper in resealable plastic food storage bag. Combine cracker crumbs and oregano in shallow bowl. Whisk together egg white and water in small bowl.

3. Place 6 or 8 chicken pieces in bag with flour mixture; seal bag. Shake bag until chicken is well coated. Remove chicken from bag, shaking off excess flour. Dip chicken pieces into egg white mixture, coating all sides. Roll in crumb mixture. Place in shallow baking pan. Repeat with remaining chicken pieces. Bake 10 to 13 minutes or until golden brown.

4. Meanwhile, stir together barbecue sauce and jam in small saucepan. Cook and stir over low heat until heated through. (If freezing nuggets, do not prepare dipping sauce at this time.) Serve chicken nuggets with dipping sauce or follow directions for freezing and reheating. *makes 8 servings*

note: To freeze chicken nuggets, cool 5 minutes on baking sheet. Wrap chicken in plastic wrap, making packages of 4 to 5 nuggets each. Place packages in freezer container or plastic freezer bag. Freeze. To reheat nuggets, preheat oven to 325°F. Unwrap nuggets. Place nuggets on ungreased baking sheet. Bake for 13 to 15 minutes or until hot. Or, place 4 to 5 nuggets on microwavable plate. Heat on DEFROST (30% power) for 2½ to 3½ minutes or until hot, turning once.

For each serving, stir together about 1½ teaspoons barbecue sauce and ½ teaspoon jam in small microwavable dish. Heat on HIGH 10 to 15 seconds or until hot.

grilled cheese & turkey shapes

8 teaspoons *French's®* **Mustard, any flavor**

8 slices seedless rye or sourdough bread

8 slices deli roast turkey

4 slices American cheese

2 tablespoons butter or margarine, softened

1. Spread *1 teaspoon* mustard on each slice of bread. Arrange turkey and cheese on half of the bread slices, dividing evenly. Cover with top halves of bread.

2. Cut out sandwich shapes using choice of cookie cutters. Place cookie cutter on top of sandwich; press down firmly. Remove excess trimmings.

3. Spread butter on both sides of bread. Heat large nonstick skillet over medium heat. Cook sandwiches 1 minute per side or until bread is golden and cheese melts.   *makes 4 sandwiches*

tip: Use 2½-inch star, heart, teddy-bear or flower-shaped cookie cutters.

prep time: 15 minutes
cook time: 2 minutes

Kids love these sandwiches, so if you find that you're serving them often, try varying the sandwich ingredients from time to time. Substitute deli sliced ham for turkey, and use Cheddar, Swiss or mozzarella cheese instead of American cheese for a change of pace.

62

quick and easy italian sandwich

1 tablespoon olive or vegetable oil

½ pound mild Italian sausage, casing removed, sliced ½ inch thick

1 can (14.5 ounces) CONTADINA® Recipe Ready Diced Tomatoes with Italian Herbs, undrained

½ cup sliced green bell pepper

6 sandwich-size English muffins, split, toasted

¼ cup (1 ounce) shredded Parmesan cheese, divided

1. Heat oil in medium skillet. Add sausage; cook 3 to 4 minutes or until no longer pink in center, stirring occasionally. Drain.

2. Add undrained tomatoes and bell pepper; simmer, uncovered, 5 minutes, stirring occasionally.

3. Spread ½ cup meat mixture on each of 6 muffin halves; sprinkle with Parmesan cheese. Top with remaining muffin halves.

makes 6 servings

It's more economical to purchase a chunk of cheese and grate it yourself than to buy already grated cheese. (It also lasts longer.) Hard cheeses like Parmesan can be grated on a flat metal grater with small holes, a box grater or a hand-held rotary grater.

piñata twirls

1 cup UNCLE BEN'S® ORIGINAL CONVERTED® Brand Rice

1 package (1 pound) TYSON® Fresh Ground Chicken

1 jar (16 ounces) chunky salsa

1½ cups corn (frozen, fresh or canned, drained)

16 (8-inch) whole wheat flour tortillas, warmed

1 cup shredded Colby-Jack cheese

COOK: Prepare rice according to package directions. CLEAN: Wash hands. In large nonstick skillet, cook chicken over medium-high heat 6 to 8 minutes or until no longer pink. Stir in salsa, cooked rice and corn. Simmer 5 minutes or until liquid is absorbed. Spoon ⅓ cup mixture onto warm tortilla; top with 1 tablespoon cheese. Tightly roll tortilla to serve.

SERVE: Serve with chips and salsa, if desired.

CHILL: Refrigerate leftovers immediately.   *makes 8 servings*

prep time: none
cook time: 35 minutes

corn dogs

8 hot dogs

8 wooden craft sticks

1 package (about 16 ounces) refrigerated grand-size corn biscuits

⅓ cup *French's*® Classic Yellow® Mustard

8 slices American cheese, cut in half

1. Preheat oven to 350°F. Insert 1 wooden craft stick halfway into each hot dog; set aside.

2. Separate biscuits. On floured board, press or roll each biscuit into a 7×4-inch oval. Spread *2 teaspoons* mustard lengthwise down center of each biscuit. Top each with 2 pieces of cheese. Place hot dog in center of biscuit. Fold top of dough over end of hot dog. Fold sides towards center enclosing hot dog. Pinch edges to seal.

3. Place corn dogs, seam-side down, on greased baking sheet. Bake 20 to 25 minutes or until golden brown. Cool slightly before serving.

makes 8 servings

tip: Corn dogs may be made without wooden craft sticks.

prep time: 15 minutes
cook time: 20 minutes

cheeseburger soup

½ pound ground beef

3½ cups water

½ cup cherry tomato halves or chopped tomato

1 pouch LIPTON® Soup Secrets Ring-O-Noodle Soup Mix with Real Chicken Broth

4 ounces Cheddar cheese, shredded

Shape ground beef into 16 mini burgers.

In large saucepan, thoroughly brown burgers; drain. Add water, tomatoes and soup mix; bring to a boil. Reduce heat and simmer uncovered, stirring occasionally, 5 minutes or until burgers are cooked and noodles are tender. Stir in cheese.

makes about 4 (1-cup) servings

66

rock 'n' rollers

4 (6- to 7-inch) flour tortillas

4 ounces reduced-fat cream cheese, softened

⅓ cup peach preserves

1 cup (4 ounces) shredded Cheddar cheese

½ cup packed washed fresh spinach leaves

3 ounces thinly sliced regular or smoked turkey breast

1. Spread each tortilla evenly with 1 ounce cream cheese; cover with thin layer of preserves. Sprinkle with Cheddar cheese.

2. Arrange spinach leaves and turkey over Cheddar cheese. Roll up tortillas; trim ends. Cover and refrigerate until ready to serve.

3. Cut "rollers" crosswise in half or diagonally into 1-inch pieces.

makes 8 servings

sassy salsa rollers: Substitute salsa for peach preserves and shredded iceberg lettuce for spinach leaves.

ham 'n' apple rollers: Omit peach preserves and spinach leaves. Substitute lean ham slices for turkey. Spread tortillas with cream cheese as directed; sprinkle with Cheddar cheese. Top each tortilla with about 2 tablespoons finely chopped apple and 2 ham slices; roll up. Continue as directed.

wedgies: Prepare Rock 'n' Rollers or any variation as directed, but do not roll up. Top with a second tortilla; cut into wedges.

69

ultimate grilled cheese

2 slices bread

2 ounces VELVEETA® Pasteurized Prepared Cheese Product, sliced

2 teaspoons soft margarine

1. Top 1 bread slice with Velveeta and second bread slice.

2. Spread outside of sandwich with margarine.

3. Cook in skillet on medium heat until lightly browned on both sides.

makes 1 sandwich

prep time: 5 minutes
cook time: 10 minutes

cheeseburger calzones

1 pound ground beef

1 medium onion, chopped

½ teaspoon salt

1 jar (26 to 28 ounces) RAGÚ® Hearty Robusto!™ Pasta Sauce

1 jar (8 ounces) marinated mushrooms, drained and chopped (optional)

1 cup shredded Cheddar cheese (about 4 ounces)

1 package (2 pounds) frozen pizza dough, thawed

1. Preheat oven to 375°F. In 12-inch skillet, brown ground beef with onion and salt over medium-high heat; drain. Stir in 1 cup Ragú® Hearty Robusto! Pasta Sauce, mushrooms and cheese.

2. On floured board, cut each pound of dough into 4 pieces; press to form 6-inch circles. Spread ½ cup beef mixture on each dough circle; fold over and pinch edges to close.

3. With large spatula, gently arrange on cookie sheets. Bake 25 minutes or until golden. Serve with remaining sauce, heated.

makes 8 servings

prep time: 15 minutes
cook time: 25 minutes

70

sub on the run

- 2 hard rolls, split into halves
- 4 tomato slices
- 14 turkey pepperoni slices
- 2 ounces fat-free oven-roasted turkey breast
- ¼ cup (1 ounce) shredded part-skim mozzarella or reduced-fat sharp Cheddar cheese
- 1 cup packaged coleslaw mix or shredded lettuce
- ¼ medium green bell pepper, thinly sliced (optional)
- 2 tablespoons prepared fat-free Italian salad dressing

Top each of the two bottom halves of rolls with 2 tomato slices, 7 pepperoni slices, half of turkey, 2 tablespoons cheese, ½ cup coleslaw mix and half of bell pepper slices, if desired. Drizzle with salad dressing. Top with roll tops. Cut into halves, if desired.

makes 2 servings

Subs make great party food for kids! To make a party-sized sub, purchase long French or Italian breads at the supermarket and inrease the quantity of sandwich ingredients according to how many kids you'll be serving. Or, purchase round loaves of bread and cut the sandwich into wedges instead.

72

tuna monte cristo sandwiches

4 thin slices (2 ounces) Cheddar cheese

4 oval slices sourdough or challah (egg) bread

½ pound deli tuna salad

1 egg, beaten

¼ cup milk

2 tablespoons butter or margarine

1. Place 1 slice cheese on each bread slice. Spread tuna salad evenly over two slices of cheese-topped bread. Close sandwich with remaining bread.

2. Combine egg and milk in shallow bowl. Dip sandwiches in egg mixture, turning to coat well.

3. Melt butter in large nonstick skillet over medium heat. Add sandwiches; cook 4 to 5 minutes per side or until golden brown and cheese is melted. *makes 2 servings*

serving suggestion: Serve with a chilled fruit salad.

prep and cook time: 20 minutes

zesty chicken & vegetable soup

½ pound boneless skinless chicken breasts, cut into very thin strips

1 to 2 tablespoons *Frank's® RedHot®* Sauce

4 cups chicken broth

1 package (16 ounces) frozen stir-fry vegetables

1 cup angel hair pasta, broken into 2-inch lengths *or* fine egg noodles

1 green onion, thinly sliced

1. Combine chicken and *RedHot* Sauce in medium bowl; set aside.

2. Heat broth to boiling in large saucepan over medium-high heat. Add vegetables and noodles; return to boiling. Cook 2 minutes. Stir in chicken mixture and green onion. Cook 1 minute or until chicken is no longer pink. *makes 4 to 6 servings*

tip: For a change of pace, substitute 6 prepared frozen pot stickers for the pasta. Add to broth in step 2 and boil until tender.

prep time: 5 minutes
cook time: about 8 minutes

rainbow spirals

4 (10-inch) flour tortillas
(assorted flavors
and colors)

4 tablespoons *French's*®
Mustard (any flavor)

½ pound (about 8 slices)
thinly sliced deli
roast beef, bologna
or turkey

8 slices American,
provolone or
Muenster cheese

Fancy party
toothpicks

1. Spread each tortilla with *1 tablespoon* mustard. Layer with meat and cheese, dividing evenly.

2. Roll-up jelly-roll style; secure with toothpicks and cut into thirds. Arrange on platter.

makes 4 to 6 servings

prep time: 10 minutes

quick corn bread with chilies 'n' cheese

1 package (12 to
16 ounces) corn
bread or corn
muffin mix

1 cup (4 ounces)
shredded Monterey
Jack cheese

1 can (4 ounces)
chopped green
chilies, drained

1 envelope LIPTON®
RECIPE SECRETS®
Vegetable Soup Mix

Prepare corn bread mix according to package directions; stir in ½ cup cheese, chilies and vegetable soup mix. Pour batter into lightly greased 8-inch baking pan; bake as directed. While warm, top with remaining cheese. Cool completely on wire rack. To serve, cut into squares.

makes 16 servings

perfect pita pizzas

2 whole wheat or white pita bread rounds

½ cup spaghetti or pizza sauce

¾ cup (3 ounces) shredded part-skim mozzarella cheese

1 small zucchini, sliced ¼ inch thick

½ small carrot, peeled and sliced

2 cherry tomatoes, halved

¼ small green bell pepper, sliced

1. Preheat oven to 375°F. Line baking sheet with foil; set aside.

2. Using small scissors, carefully split each pita bread round around edge; separate to form 2 rounds.

3. Place rounds, rough sides up, on prepared baking sheet. Bake 5 minutes.

4. Spread 2 tablespoons spaghetti sauce onto each round; sprinkle with cheese. Decorate with vegetables to create faces. Bake 10 to 12 minutes or until cheese melts. *makes 4 servings*

pepperoni pita pizzas: Prepare pita rounds, partially bake and top with spaghetti sauce and cheese as directed. Place 2 small pepperoni slices on each pizza for eyes. Decorate with cut-up fresh vegetables for rest of face. Continue to bake as directed.

festive franks

1 can (8 ounces) reduced-fat crescent roll dough

5½ teaspoons barbecue sauce

⅓ cup finely shredded reduced-fat sharp Cheddar cheese

8 fat-free hot dogs

¼ teaspoon poppy seeds (optional)

Additional barbecue sauce (optional)

1. Preheat oven to 350°F. Spray large baking sheet with nonstick cooking spray; set aside.

2. Unroll dough and separate into 8 triangles. Cut each triangle in half lengthwise to make 2 triangles. Lightly spread barbecue sauce over each triangle. Sprinkle with cheese.

3. Cut each hot dog in half; trim off rounded ends. Place one hot dog piece at large end of one dough triangle. Roll up jelly-roll style from wide end. Place point-side down on prepared baking sheet. Sprinkle with poppy seeds, if desired. Repeat with remaining hot dog pieces and dough.

4. Bake 13 minutes or until dough is golden brown. Cool 1 to 2 minutes on baking sheet. Serve with additional barbecue sauce for dipping, if desired. *makes 16 servings*

aquarium cups

¾ cup boiling water

1 package (4-serving size) JELL-O® Brand Berry Blue Flavor Gelatin Dessert

½ cup cold water

Ice cubes

Gummy fish

STIR boiling water into gelatin in medium bowl at least 2 minutes until completely dissolved. Mix cold water and ice cubes to make 1¼ cups. Add to gelatin, stirring until slightly thickened. Remove any remaining ice. (If mixture is still thin, refrigerate until slightly thickened.)

POUR thickened gelatin into 4 dessert dishes. Suspend gummy fish in gelatin. Refrigerate 1 hour or until firm. *makes 4 servings*

preparation time: 10 minutes
refrigerating time: 1 hour

bread pudding snacks

1¼ cups reduced-fat (2%) milk

½ cup egg substitute

⅓ cup sugar

1 teaspoon vanilla

⅛ teaspoon salt

⅛ teaspoon ground nutmeg (optional)

4 cups (½-inch) cinnamon or cinnamon-raisin bread cubes (about 6 bread slices)

1 tablespoon margarine or butter, melted

1. Combine milk, egg substitute, sugar, vanilla, salt and nutmeg in medium bowl; mix well. Add bread; mix until well moistened. Let stand at room temperature 15 minutes.

2. Preheat oven to 350°F. Line 12 medium-sized muffin cups with paper liners.

3. Spoon bread mixture evenly into prepared cups; drizzle evenly with margarine.

4. Bake 30 to 35 minutes or until snacks are puffed and golden brown. Remove to wire rack to cool completely. *makes 12 servings*

note: Snacks will puff up in the oven and fall slightly upon cooling.

caramel dip

1 tub (8 ounces) COOL WHIP® Whipped Topping, thawed

¾ cup KRAFT® Caramel-Flavored Dessert Topping

Assorted cut-up fruits (such as apples, pears and bananas)

Assorted cookies

GENTLY stir whipped topping and caramel topping in large bowl.

SERVE dip with fruit and cookies. *makes about 3 cups*

prep time: 5 minutes

easy pudding milk shake

3 cups cold milk

1 package (4-serving size) JELL-O® Instant Pudding & Pie Filling, any flavor

1½ cups ice cream, any flavor

POUR milk into blender container. Add pudding mix and ice cream; cover. Blend on high speed 30 seconds or until smooth. Pour into glasses and garnish as desired. Serve immediately.

makes 5 servings

preparation time: 5 minutes

berry striped pops

2 cups strawberries

¾ cup honey,* divided

6 kiwifruit, peeled and sliced

2 cups sliced peaches

12 (3-ounce) paper cups or popsicle molds

12 popsicle sticks

Honey should not be fed to infants under one year of age. Honey is a safe and wholesome food for older children and adults.

Purée strawberries with ¼ cup honey in blender or food processor. Divide mixture evenly between 12 cups or popsicle molds. Freeze about 30 minutes or until firm. Meanwhile, rinse processor; purée kiwifruit with ¼ cup honey. Repeat process with peaches and remaining ¼ cup honey. When strawberry layer is firm, pour kiwifruit purée into molds. Insert popsicle sticks and freeze about 30 minutes or until firm. Pour peach purée into molds and freeze until firm and ready to serve.

makes 12 servings

Favorite recipe from **National Honey Board**

cocoa snackin' jacks

1 (3-ounce) bag ORVILLE REDENBACHER'S® Microwave Popping Corn, popped according to package instructions

½ cup crumbled reduced fat chocolate cookies

½ cup granulated sugar

½ cup firmly packed brown sugar

¼ cup light corn syrup

2 tablespoons reduced fat margarine

1 tablespoon water

¼ teaspoon cream of tartar

1 (.53-oz) package SWISS MISS® Fat Free Hot Cocoa Mix

1 teaspoon baking soda

1. In large bowl, combine Orville Redenbacher's Popped Corn and cookies; set aside.

2. In medium saucepan, combine sugars, syrup, margarine, water and cream of tartar.

3. Bring to a boil and stir constantly until thermometer reaches 260°F. Remove from heat.

4. Quickly add Swiss Miss Cocoa and baking soda; stir thoroughly.

5. Working quickly, pour mixture over popcorn and cookie mixture. Gently toss to coat.

6. Spread mixture onto waxed paper to cool and harden. Break into pieces.   *makes 16 (1-ounce) servings*

To soften brown sugar that has hardened, place 1 cup of brown sugar in a microwavable bowl and cover with plastic wrap. Heat at High 30 to 45 seconds; stir and repeat if necessary. Watch the brown sugar carefully to make sure it doesn't melt.

cheddary pull apart bread

1 round loaf corn or
    sourdough bread
    (1 pound)*

½ cup (1 stick) butter or
    margarine, melted

¼ cup *French's*® Classic
    Yellow® Mustard

½ teaspoon chili powder

½ teaspoon seasoned
    salt

¼ teaspoon garlic
    powder

1 cup (4 ounces)
    shredded Cheddar
    cheese

*You may substitute one 12-inch
loaf Italian bread for the corn
bread.*

Cut bread into 1-inch slices, cutting about ⅔ of the way down through loaf. (Do not cut through bottom crust.) Turn bread ¼ turn and cut across slices in similar fashion. Combine butter, mustard and seasonings in small bowl until blended. Brush cut surfaces of bread with butter mixture. Spread bread "sticks" apart and sprinkle cheese inside. Wrap loaf in foil.

Place packet on grid. Cook over medium coals about 30 minutes or until bread is toasted and cheese melts. Pull bread "sticks" apart to serve. *makes about 8 servings*

prep time: 15 minutes
cook time: 30 minutes

pepperoni pizza dip

1 cup RAGÚ® Old World
    Style® Pasta Sauce

1 cup RAGÚ® Cheese
    Creations!® Classic
    Alfredo Sauce

1 cup shredded
    mozzarella cheese
    (about 4 ounces)

¼ to ½ cup finely
    chopped pepperoni

1. In 2-quart saucepan, heat Ragú Pasta Sauces, cheese and pepperoni, stirring occasionally, 10 minutes or until cheese is melted.

2. Pour into 1½-quart casserole or serving dish and serve, if desired, with breadsticks, sliced Italian bread or crackers.

makes 3½ cups dip

prep time: 5 minutes
cook time: 10 minutes

kids' quesadillas

8 slices American cheese

8 (10-inch) flour tortillas

6 tablespoons *French's®* Honey Mustard

½ pound thinly sliced deli turkey

2 tablespoons melted butter

¼ teaspoon paprika

1. To prepare 1 quesadilla, arrange 2 slices of cheese on 1 tortilla. Top with one-fourth of the turkey. Spread with *1½ tablespoons* mustard, then top with another tortilla. Prepare 3 more quesadillas with remaining ingredients.

2. Combine butter and paprika. Brush one side of tortilla with butter mixture. Preheat 12-inch nonstick skillet over medium-high heat. Arrange tortilla butter side down and cook 2 minutes. Brush tortilla with butter mixture and turn over. Cook 1½ minutes or until golden brown. Repeat with remaining three quesadillas.

3. Slice into wedges before serving. *makes 4 servings*

prep time: 5 minutes
cook time: 15 minutes

creamy hot chocolate

1 (14-ounce) can EAGLE® BRAND Sweetened Condensed Milk (NOT evaporated milk)

½ cup unsweetened cocoa

1½ teaspoons vanilla extract

⅛ teaspoon salt

6½ cups hot water

Marshmallows (optional)

1. In large saucepan over medium heat, combine Eagle Brand, cocoa, vanilla and salt; mix well.

2. Slowly stir in water. Heat through, stirring occasionally. Do not boil. Top with marshmallows, if desired. Store covered in refrigerator.

makes about 2 quarts

microwave directions: In 2-quart glass measure, combine all ingredients except marshmallows. Microwave on 100% power (HIGH) 8 to 10 minutes, stirring every 3 minutes. Top with marshmallows, if desired. Store covered in refrigerator.

tip: Hot chocolate can be stored in refrigerator up to 5 days. Mix well and reheat before serving.

prep time: 8 to 10 minutes

creamy taco dip

1 pound (16 ounces) VELVEETA® Pasteurized Prepared Cheese Product, cut up

1 container (16 ounces) BREAKSTONE'S® or KNUDSEN® Sour Cream

1 package (1¼ ounces) TACO BELL® HOME ORIGINALS™* Taco Seasoning Mix*

*TACO BELL and HOME ORIGINALS are registered trademarks owned and licensed by Taco Bell Corp.

1. Microwave all ingredients in 2-quart microwavable bowl on HIGH 5 minutes or until Velveeta is melted, stirring after 3 minutes. Serve hot or cold with corn chips or tortilla chips. *makes 3½ cups*

prep time: 5 minutes
microwave time: 5 minutes

banana tot pops

3 firm, medium DOLE® Bananas

6 large wooden sticks

½ cup raspberry or other flavored yogurt

1 jar (1¾ ounces) chocolate or rainbow sprinkles

• Cut each banana crosswise in half. Insert wooden stick into each half.

• Pour yogurt into small bowl. Hold banana pop over bowl; spoon yogurt to cover all sides of banana. Allow excess yogurt to drip into bowl. Sprinkle candies over yogurt.

• Place pops on wax paper lined tray. Freeze 2 hours.

makes 6 servings

prep time: 20 minutes
freeze time: 2 hours

90

one potato, two potato

Nonstick cooking
spray

2 medium baking
potatoes, cut
lengthwise into
4 wedges

Salt

½ cup unseasoned dry
bread crumbs

2 tablespoons grated
Parmesan cheese
(optional)

1½ teaspoons dried
oregano leaves, dill
weed, Italian herbs
or paprika

Spicy brown or honey
mustard, ketchup or
reduced-fat sour
cream

1. Preheat oven to 425°F. Spray baking sheet with nonstick cooking spray; set aside.

2. Spray cut sides of potatoes generously with cooking spray; sprinkle lightly with salt.

3. Combine bread crumbs, Parmesan cheese and desired herb in shallow dish. Add potatoes; toss lightly until potatoes are generously coated with crumb mixture. Place on prepared baking sheet.

4. Bake potatoes until browned and tender, about 20 minutes. Serve warm as dippers with mustard. *makes 4 servings*

potato sweets: Omit Parmesan cheese, herbs and mustard. Substitute sweet potatoes for baking potatoes. Cut and spray potatoes as directed; coat generously with desired amount of cinnamon-sugar. Bake as directed. Serve warm as dippers with peach or pineapple preserves or honey mustard.

choco-nutty shakes

1½ cups COOL WHIP®
Whipped Topping,
not thawed

1 cup cold milk

¼ cup chocolate syrup

¼ cup creamy peanut
butter

PLACE frozen whipped topping, milk, chocolate syrup and peanut butter in blender container; cover. Blend on high speed until smooth. Serve immediately. *makes 2 servings*

92

cinnamon-raisin roll-ups

4 ounces reduced-fat cream cheese, softened

½ cup shredded carrot

¼ cup raisins

1 tablespoon honey

¼ teaspoon ground cinnamon

4 (7- to 8-inch) whole wheat or regular flour tortillas

8 thin apple wedges

1. Combine cream cheese, carrot, raisins, honey and cinnamon in small bowl; mix well.

2. Spread tortillas evenly with cream cheese mixture, leaving ½-inch border around edge of each tortilla. Place 2 apple wedges down center of each tortilla; roll up. Wrap in plastic wrap. Refrigerate until ready to serve or pack in lunch box. *makes 4 servings*

cook's tip: For extra convenience, prepare roll-ups the night before. In the morning, pack roll-up in lunch box along with a frozen juice box. The juice box will be thawed by lunchtime and will keep the snack cold in the meantime!

tuna 'n' celery sticks

4 ounces cream cheese, softened

3 tablespoons plain yogurt or mayonnaise

1½ teaspoons dried basil

1 can (12 ounces) STARKIST® Solid White or Chunk Light Tuna, drained and flaked

½ cup finely grated carrot or zucchini

½ cup finely shredded Cheddar cheese

2 teaspoons instant minced onion

10 to 12 celery stalks, cleaned

In large bowl, mix together cream cheese, yogurt and basil until smooth. Add tuna, carrot, Cheddar cheese and onion; mix well. Spread mixture into celery stalks; cut into fourths. *makes 40 servings*

prep time: 10 minutes

94

herb cheese twists

2 tablespoons butter or margarine

¼ cup grated Parmesan cheese

1 teaspoon dried parsley flakes

1 teaspoon dried basil leaves

1 can (7½ ounces) refrigerated buttermilk biscuits

1. Preheat oven to 400°F. Microwave butter in small bowl at 50% power just until melted; cool slightly. Stir in cheese, parsley and basil. Set aside.

2. Pat each biscuit into 5×2-inch rectangle. Spread 1 teaspoon of butter mixture on each rectangle; cut each in half lengthwise. Twist each strip 3 or 4 times. Place on lightly greased baking sheet. Bake 8 to 10 minutes or until golden brown. *makes 5 servings*

cut the time: Butter mixture can be spread on ready-to-bake bread sticks and baked according to package directions.

prep and cook time: 20 minutes

chocolate-peanut butter-apple treats

½ (8-ounce package) fat-free or reduced-fat cream cheese, softened

¼ cup reduced-fat chunky peanut butter

2 tablespoons mini chocolate chips

2 large apples

1. Combine cream cheese, peanut butter and chocolate chips in small bowl; mix well.

2. Cut each apple into 12 wedges; discard stems and seeds. Spread about 1½ teaspoons of the mixture over each apple slice.

makes 8 servings (4 apple wedges and 1½ teaspoons spread)

nachos à la ortega®

1¾ cups (1-pound can) ORTEGA® Refried Beans, warmed

4 cups (4 ounces) baked tortilla chips

1½ cups (6 ounces) shredded Monterey Jack cheese

2 tablespoons ORTEGA® Sliced Jalapeños

ORTEGA® Thick & Chunky Salsa, (optional)

Sour cream (optional)

Additional topping suggestions: guacamole, sliced ripe olives, chopped green onions, chopped fresh cilantro (optional)

PREHEAT broiler.

SPREAD beans over bottom of large ovenproof platter or 15×10-inch jelly-roll pan. Arrange chips over beans. Top with cheese and jalapeños.

BROIL for 1 to 1½ minutes or until cheese is melted. Top with salsa and sour cream.   *makes 4 to 6 servings*

Refried beans are made with red beans or pinto beans that are mashed and then fried (only once). They are often prepared with lard or beef flavoring, but vegetarian versions are also available, as well as flavored and fat-free varieties.

98

purple cow jumped over the moon

3 cups vanilla nonfat frozen yogurt

1 cup reduced-fat (2%) milk

½ cup thawed frozen grape juice concentrate (undiluted)

1½ teaspoons lemon juice

Place yogurt, milk, grape juice concentrate and lemon juice in food processor or blender container; process until smooth. Serve immediately.

makes 8 (½-cup) servings

razzmatazz shake: Place 1 quart vanilla nonfat frozen yogurt, 1 cup vanilla nonfat yogurt and ¼ cup fat-free chocolate syrup in food processor or blender container; process until smooth. Pour ½ of mixture evenly into 12 glasses; top with ½ of (12-ounce) can root beer. Fill glasses equally with remaining yogurt mixture; top with remaining root beer. Makes 12 (⅔-cup) servings.

sunshine shake: Place 1 quart vanilla nonfat frozen yogurt, 1⅓ cups orange juice, 1 cup fresh or thawed frozen raspberries and 1 teaspoon sugar in food processor or blender container; process until smooth. Pour into 10 glasses; sprinkle with ground nutmeg. Makes 10 (½-cup) servings.

taco bread

1 loaf frozen bread dough, thawed

1½ cups (6 ounces) shredded cheddar cheese

1 package (1.0 ounce) LAWRY'S® Taco Spices & Seasonings

3 tablespoons butter or margarine, melted

On baking sheet, stretch dough into 14×8-inch rectangle. Sprinkle with cheese and Taco Seasoning Mix; drizzle with margarine. Roll up jelly roll fashion (lengthwise); place seam side down on baking sheet. Bake, uncovered, in 350°F oven 20 to 25 minutes until golden brown.

makes 6 servings

serving suggestions: Slice bread when cooled and serve as a spicy addition to hearty soups.

honey popcorn clusters

Vegetable cooking spray

6 cups air-popped popcorn

⅔ cup DOLE® Golden or Seedless Raisins

½ cup DOLE® Chopped Dates or Pitted Dates, chopped

⅓ cup almonds (optional)

⅓ cup packed brown sugar

¼ cup honey

2 tablespoons margarine

¼ teaspoon baking soda

• Line bottom and sides of 13×9-inch baking pan with large sheet of aluminum foil. Spray foil with vegetable cooking spray.

• Stir together popcorn, raisins, dates and almonds in foil-lined pan.

• Combine brown sugar, honey and margarine in small saucepan. Bring to boil over medium heat, stirring constantly; reduce heat to low. Cook 5 minutes. *Do not stir.* Remove from heat.

• Stir in baking soda. Pour evenly over popcorn mixture, stirring quickly to coat mixture evenly.

• Bake at 300°F 12 to 15 minutes or until mixture is lightly browned, stirring once halfway through baking time.

• Lift foil from pan; place on cooling rack. Cool popcorn mixture completely; break into clusters. Popcorn clusters can be stored in airtight container up to 1 week.   *makes 7 cups*

prep time: 20 minutes
bake time: 15 minutes

philadelphia® fruit dip

1 package (8 ounces) PHILADELPHIA® Cream Cheese, softened

1 container (8 ounces) strawberry *or* any flavored yogurt

MIX cream cheese and yogurt with electric mixer on medium speed until well blended. Refrigerate.

SERVE with assorted fresh fruit.   *makes about 1⅔ cups*

prep: 5 minutes plus refrigerating

teddy bear party mix

4 cups crisp cinnamon graham cereal

2 cups honey flavored teddy-shaped graham snacks

1 can (1½ ounces) *French's*® Potato Sticks

3 tablespoons melted unsalted butter

2 tablespoons *French's*® Worcestershire Sauce

1 tablespoon packed brown sugar

¼ teaspoon ground cinnamon

1 cup sweetened dried cranberries or raisins

½ cup chocolate, peanut butter or carob chips

1. Preheat oven to 350°F. Lightly spray jelly-roll pan with nonstick cooking spray. Combine cereal, graham snacks and potato sticks in large bowl.

2. Combine butter, Worcestershire, sugar and cinnamon in small bowl; toss with cereal mixture. Transfer to prepared pan. Bake 12 minutes. Cool completely.

3. Stir in dried cranberries and chips. Store in an airtight container.

makes about 7 cups

prep time: 5 minutes
cook time: 12 minutes

pizza snack cups

1 can (12 ounces)
   refrigerated biscuits
   (10 biscuits)
½ pound ground beef
1 jar (14 ounces) RAGÚ®
   Pizza Quick® Sauce
½ cup shredded
   mozzarella cheese
   (about 2 ounces)

1. Preheat oven to 375°F. In 12-cup muffin pan, evenly press each biscuit in bottom and up side of each cup; chill until ready to fill.

2. In 10-inch skillet, brown ground beef over medium-high heat; drain. Stir in Ragú Pizza Quick Sauce and heat through.

3. Evenly spoon beef mixture into prepared muffin cups. Bake 15 minutes. Sprinkle with cheese and bake an additional 5 minutes or until cheese is melted and biscuits are golden. Let stand 5 minutes. Gently remove pizza cups from muffin pan and serve.

makes 10 pizza cups

prep time: 10 minutes
cook time: 25 minutes

take-along snack mix

1 tablespoon butter or
   margarine
2 tablespoons honey
1 cup toasted oat
   cereal, any flavor
½ cup coarsely broken
   pecans
½ cup thin pretzel sticks,
   broken in half
½ cup raisins
1 cup "M&M's"®
   Chocolate Mini
   Baking Bits

In large heavy skillet over low heat, melt butter; add honey and stir until blended. Add cereal, nuts, pretzels and raisins, stirring until all pieces are evenly coated. Continue cooking over low heat about 10 minutes, stirring frequently. Remove from heat; immediately spread on waxed paper until cool. Add "M&M's"® Chocolate Mini Baking Bits. Store in tightly covered container.

makes about 3½ cups

fantasy cinnamon applewiches

4 raisin bread slices

⅓ cup reduced-fat cream cheese

¼ cup finely chopped unpeeled apple

1 teaspoon sugar

⅛ teaspoon ground cinnamon

1. Toast bread. Cut into desired shapes using large cookie cutters.

2. Combine cream cheese and apple in small bowl; spread onto toast.

3. Combine sugar and cinnamon in another small bowl; sprinkle evenly over cream cheese mixture. *makes 4 servings*

cook's tip: Get out the cookie cutters any time of the year for this fun treat. Or, create your own fun shapes—be sure to have an adult cut out the requested shapes with a serrated knife for best results.

savory cheddar bread

2 cups all-purpose flour

4 teaspoons baking powder

1 tablespoon sugar

½ teaspoon onion salt

½ teaspoon oregano, crushed

¼ teaspoon dry mustard

1 cup (4 ounces) SARGENTO® Fancy Mild or Sharp Cheddar Shredded Cheese

1 egg, beaten

1 cup milk

1 tablespoon butter or margarine, melted

In large bowl, stir together flour, baking powder, sugar, onion salt, oregano, dry mustard and cheese. In separate bowl, combine egg, milk and butter; add to dry ingredients, stirring just until moistened. Spread batter in greased 8×4-inch loaf pan. Bake at 350°F 45 minutes or until wooden pick inserted in center comes out clean. Cool 10 minutes on wire rack. Remove from pan. *makes 16 slices*

ranch baked quesadillas

1 cup shredded cooked chicken

1 cup (4 ounces) shredded Monterey Jack cheese

½ cup HIDDEN VALLEY® Original Ranch® Dressing

¼ cup diced green chiles, rinsed and drained

4 (9-inch) flour tortillas, heated

Salsa and guacamole (optional)

Combine chicken, cheese, dressing and chiles in a medium bowl. Place about ½ cup chicken mixture on each tortilla; fold in half. Place quesadillas on a baking sheet. Bake at 350°F. for 15 minutes or until cheese is melted. Cut into thirds, if desired. Serve with salsa and guacamole, if desired.

makes 4 servings

rocky road popcorn balls

6 cups unbuttered popped popcorn, lightly salted

2 cups "M&M's"® Chocolate Mini Baking Bits, divided

1¾ cups peanuts

¼ cup (½ stick) butter

4 cups miniature marshmallows, divided

In large bowl combine popcorn, 1½ cups "M&M's"® Chocolate Mini Baking Bits and peanuts; set aside. Place remaining ½ cup "M&M's"® Chocolate Mini Baking Bits in shallow bowl; set aside. In large saucepan over low heat, combine butter and marshmallows until melted, stirring often. Pour marshmallow mixture over popcorn mixture; stir until well coated. Form popcorn mixture into 12 balls; roll in "M&M's"® Chocolate Mini Baking Bits. Store in tightly covered container.

makes 12 popcorn balls

berry good dip

8 ounces fresh or thawed frozen strawberries

4 ounces fat-free cream cheese, softened

¼ cup reduced-fat sour cream

1 tablespoon sugar

1. Place strawberries in food processor or blender container; process until smooth.

2. Beat cream cheese in small bowl until smooth. Stir in sour cream, strawberry purée and sugar; cover. Refrigerate until ready to serve.

3. Spoon dip into small serving bowl. Garnish with orange peel, if desired. Serve with assorted fresh fruit dippers or angel food cake cubes.

makes 6 (¼-cup) servings

tip: For a super quick fruit spread for toasted mini English muffins or bagels, beat 1 package (8 ounces) softened nonfat cream cheese in small bowl until fluffy. Stir in 3 to 4 tablespoons strawberry spreadable fruit. Season to taste with 1 to 2 teaspoons sugar, if desired. Makes 6 servings.

quick s'mores

1 whole graham cracker

1 large marshmallow

1 teaspoon hot fudge sauce

1. Break graham cracker in half crosswise. Place one half on small paper plate or microwavable plate; top with marshmallow.

2. Spread remaining ½ of cracker with fudge sauce.

3. Place cracker with marshmallow in microwave. Microwave at HIGH 12 to 14 seconds or until marshmallow puffs up. Immediately place remaining cracker, fudge side down, over marshmallow. Press crackers gently to even out marshmallow layer. Cool completely.

makes 1 serving

tip: S'mores can be made the night before and wrapped in plastic wrap or sealed in a small plastic food storage bag. Store at room temperature until ready to pack in your child's lunch box the next morning.

sweet treat tortillas

- **4 (7- to 8-inch) flour tortillas**
- **4 ounces reduced-fat cream cheese, softened**
- **¼ cup strawberry or other flavor spreadable fruit or preserves**
- **1 medium banana, peeled and chopped**

1. Spread each tortilla with 1 ounce cream cheese and 1 tablespoon spreadable fruit; top with ¼ of the banana.

2. Roll up tortillas; cut crosswise into thirds.   *makes 6 servings*

more sweet treats: Substitute your favorite chopped fruit for banana.

cinnamon-spice treats: Omit spreadable fruit and banana. Mix small amounts of sugar, ground cinnamon and nutmeg into cream cheese; spread evenly onto tortillas. Sprinkle lightly with desired amount of chopped pecans or walnuts. Top with chopped fruit, if desired; roll up. Cut crosswise into thirds.

señor nacho dip

- **4 ounces fat-free cream cheese**
- **½ cup (2 ounces) reduced-fat Cheddar cheese**
- **¼ cup mild or medium chunky salsa**
- **2 teaspoons low-fat (2%) milk**
- **4 ounces baked tortilla chips or assorted fresh vegetable dippers**

1. Combine cream cheese and Cheddar cheese in small saucepan; stir over low heat until melted. Stir in salsa and milk; heat thoroughly, stirring occasionally.

2. Transfer dip to small serving bowl. Serve with tortilla chips. Garnish with hot peppers and cilantro, if desired.   *makes 4 servings*

olé dip: Substitute reduced-fat Monterey Jack cheese or taco cheese for Cheddar cheese.

spicy mustard dip: Omit tortilla chips. Substitute 2 teaspoons spicy brown or honey mustard for salsa. Serve with fresh vegetable dippers or pretzels.

velveeta® salsa dip

1 pound (16 ounces) VELVEETA® Pasteurized Prepared Cheese Product, cut up

1 (8-ounce) jar salsa or picante sauce

• Stir Velveeta and salsa in saucepan on low heat until Velveeta is melted. Stir in cilantro, if desired.

• Serve hot with tortilla chips or cut up vegetables.   *makes 3 cups*

microwave directions: Microwave Velveeta and salsa in 1½-quart microwavable bowl on HIGH 5 minutes or until Velveeta is melted, stirring after 3 minutes. Serve as directed.

variation: Prepare Velveeta® Salsa Dip as directed, adding 1 (16-ounce) can refried beans.

variation: Prepare Velveeta® Salsa Dip as directed, adding ½ pound chorizo or hot bulk pork sausage, cooked, drained.

for quick and easy taco salad: Add 1 pound browned ground beef, drained and 1 (15-ounce) can pinto or kidney beans, drained, to Velveeta® Salsa Dip. Spoon over torn greens, tomato wedges and tortilla chips. Serve with guacamole and BREAKSTONE'S® or KNUDSEN® Sour Cream, if desired.

It's easy to make your own tortilla chips—and the kids can help too! Preheat the oven to 350°F and coat a baking sheet with olive oil cooking spray. Cut flour tortillas into strips or wedges and place them on the baking sheet in a single layer. Spray them lightly with cooking spray, sprinkle with salt (and any other favorite seasoning) and bake for 7 to 10 minutes or until the edges begin to brown.

stuffed bundles

1 package (10 ounces) refrigerated pizza dough

2 ounces lean ham or turkey ham, chopped

½ cup (2 ounces) shredded reduced-fat sharp Cheddar cheese

1. Preheat oven to 425°F. Coat nonstick 12-cup muffin pan with nonstick cooking spray.

2. Unroll dough on flat surface; cut into 12 pieces, about 4×3 inch rectangles.

3. Divide ham and cheese between dough rectangles. Bring corners of dough together, pinching to seal. Place, smooth side up, in prepared muffin cups.

4. Bake 10 to 12 minutes or until golden.   *makes 12 servings*

peanut butter-pineapple celery sticks

½ cup low-fat (1%) cottage cheese

½ cup reduced-fat peanut butter

½ cup crushed pineapple in juice, drained

12 (3-inch-long) celery sticks

Combine cottage cheese and peanut butter in food processor. Blend until smooth. Stir in pineapple. Stuff celery sticks with mixture.

makes 4 servings

serving suggestion: Substitute 2 medium apples, sliced, for celery.

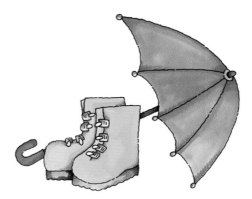

115

brontosaurus bites

4 cups air-popped popcorn

2 cups mini-dinosaur grahams

2 cups corn cereal squares

1½ cups dried pineapple wedges

1 package (6 ounces) dried fruit bits

Butter-flavored nonstick cooking spray

1 tablespoon plus 1½ teaspoons sugar

1½ teaspoons ground cinnamon

½ teaspoon ground nutmeg

1 cup yogurt-covered raisins

1. Preheat oven to 350°F. Combine popcorn, grahams, cereal, pineapple and fruit bits in large bowl; mix lightly. Transfer to 15×10-inch jelly-roll pan. Spray mixture generously with cooking spray.

2. Combine sugar, cinnamon and nutmeg in small bowl. Sprinkle ½ of sugar mixture over popcorn mixture; toss lightly to coat. Spray mixture again with additional cooking spray. Add remaining sugar mixture; mix lightly.

3. Bake snack mix 10 minutes, stirring after 5 minutes. Cool completely in pan on wire rack. Add raisins; mix lightly.

makes 12 (¾-cup) servings

gorilla grub: Substitute plain raisins for the yogurt-covered raisins and ¼ cup grated Parmesan cheese for the sugar, cinnamon and nutmeg.

tip: For individual party take-home treats, wrap snack mix in festive colored paper napkins.

116

pizza turnovers

5 ounces reduced-fat Italian bulk turkey sausage (mild)

½ cup pizza sauce

Nonstick olive oil cooking spray

1 (10-ounce) package refrigerated pizza dough

⅓ cup shredded reduced-fat Italian blend cheese

1. Preheat oven to 425°F. Cook sausage in nonstick saucepan until browned, stirring with spoon to break up meat. Drain off fat. Stir in pizza sauce. Cook until hot.

2. Spray baking sheet with cooking spray. Unroll pizza dough onto baking sheet. Pat into 12×8-inch rectangle. Cut into six (4×4-inch) squares. Divide sausage mixture evenly among squares. Sprinkle with cheese. Lift one corner of each square and fold dough over filling to opposite corner, making a triangle. Press edges with tines of fork to seal.

3. Bake 11 to 13 minutes or until golden brown. Serve immediately or follow directions for freezing and reheating. *makes 6 servings*

note: To freeze turnovers, remove to wire rack to cool for 30 minutes. Individually wrap in plastic wrap, place in freezer container or plastic freezer bag and freeze. To reheat turnovers, preheat oven to 400°F. Unwrap turnovers. Place on ungreased baking pan. Cover loosely with foil. Bake for 18 to 22 minutes or until hot. Or, place one turnover on a paper-towel-lined microwavable plate. Heat on DEFROST (30% power) 3 to 3½ minutes or until hot, turning once.

painted bread knots

1 tablespoon *French's*® Classic Yellow® Mustard

1 tablespoon milk

1 container (11 ounces) refrigerated crusty French loaf dough

Coarse salt

1. Preheat oven to 350°F. Combine mustard and milk in small bowl. Cut bread dough into 12 (1-inch) slices. Roll each slice into 8-inch long piece. Tie each into knot.

2. Arrange knots on lightly greased baking sheet. Paint each with mustard mixture. Sprinkle with salt. Bake 20 minutes or until golden. Transfer baking sheet to wire rack and let knots stand on baking sheet until completely cool.

3. Serve with additional mustard. *makes 12 servings*

prep time: 10 minutes
cook time: 20 minutes

original ranch® & cheddar bread

1 cup HIDDEN VALLEY®
Original Ranch®
Dressing

2 cups (8 ounces)
shredded sharp
Cheddar cheese

1 whole loaf (1 pound)
French bread (not
sour dough)

Stir together dressing and cheese. Cut bread in half lengthwise. Place on a broiler pan and spread dressing mixture evenly over cut side of each half. Broil until lightly brown. Cut each half into 8 pieces.

makes 16 pieces

peanut butter-banana pops

1 package (16.1 ounces)
JELL-O® No Bake
Peanut Butter Cup
Dessert

1⅓ cups cold milk

1 medium banana,
chopped

PLACE Topping Pouch in large bowl of boiling water; set aside.

POUR milk into deep, medium bowl. Add Filling Mix and Peanut Butter Packet. Beat with electric mixer on lowest speed 30 seconds. Beat on highest speed 3 minutes. (Do not underbeat.) Gently stir in Crust Mix and banana. Spoon into 12 paper-lined muffin cups.

REMOVE pouch from water. Knead pouch 60 seconds until fluid and no longer lumpy. Squeeze topping equally over mixture in cups, tilting pan slightly to coat tops. Insert pop sticks into cups.

FREEZE 2 hours or overnight until firm. Remove paper liners.

makes 12 pops

note: Wooden pop sticks are sold at craft and hobby stores.

prep time: 15 minutes
freeze time: 2 hours

120

cheesy tortilla trap™

**1 flour tortilla (6 or
  8 inches)**
**2 KRAFT® American
  Singles Pasteurized
  Process Cheese
  Food**
Salsa

• Place tortilla on microwavable plate. Place process cheese food on half of tortilla. Fold tortilla in half to cover process cheese food. Cover.

• Microwave on HIGH 25 to 40 seconds or until process cheese food begins to melt.

• Let stand, covered, 1 minute or until cool enough to eat. Fold in half again. Serve with salsa. *makes 1 serving*

top of stove: Place tortilla in medium skillet on medium heat. Place process cheese food on half of tortilla. Fold tortilla in half to cover process cheese food. Heat 1 minute on each side. Fold in half again. Serve with salsa.

oven: Heat oven to 350°F. Place process cheese food on half of tortilla. Fold tortilla in half to cover process cheese food. Bake 2 to 3 minutes or until process cheese food begins to melt. Fold in half again. Serve with salsa.

To add a burst of color and flavor to this snack, top the process cheese food with sliced red and green bell peppers. Continue cooking as directed above.

no-bake banana peanut butter fudge bars

1 ripe, large DOLE® Banana

⅔ cup butter or margarine

2 teaspoons vanilla extract

2½ cups rolled oats

½ cup packed brown sugar

1 cup semisweet chocolate chips

½ cup peanut butter

• Finely chop banana (1¼ cups). Melt butter in large skillet over medium heat; stir in vanilla. Add oats and brown sugar. Heat and stir 5 minutes. Set aside ¾ cup oat mixture. Press remaining oat mixture into greased 9-inch square baking pan. Sprinkle banana over crust.

• Melt chocolate chips and peanut butter together over low heat. Pour and spread over banana. Sprinkle with reserved oat mixture; press down lightly. Chill 2 hours before cutting. Store in refrigerator.

makes 24 bars

creamy ranch dip

1 package (8 ounces) PHILADELPHIA® Cream Cheese, softened

½ cup KRAFT® Ranch Dressing

2 tablespoons milk

MIX all ingredients with electric mixer on medium speed until smooth. Refrigerate.

SERVE with potato chips, tortilla chips or crackers. *makes 1½ cups*

bacon & ranch dip: Mix ¼ cup OSCAR MAYER® Bacon Bits into cream cheese mixture before refrigerating.

prep: 5 minutes plus refrigerating

oreo® hot cocoa

10 OREO® Chocolate
   Sandwich Cookies,
   coarsely chopped

3 cups milk

½ cup chocolate-
   flavored syrup

½ cup JET-PUFFED®
   Miniature
   Marshmallows

1. Blend chopped cookies, milk and syrup in blender until smooth.

2. Pour into 2-quart saucepan. Heat over medium-high heat, stirring frequently until hot.

3. Ladle into 4 mugs. Top with marshmallows; serve immediately.

makes 4 servings

preparation time: 15 minutes
cook time: 5 minutes
total time: 20 minutes

inside-out turkey sandwiches

2 tablespoons fat-free
   cream cheese

2 tablespoons
   pasteurized process
   cheese spread

2 teaspoons chopped
   green onion tops

1 teaspoon prepared
   mustard

12 thin round slices fat-
   free turkey breast
   or smoked turkey
   breast

4 large pretzel logs or
   unsalted bread
   sticks

1. Combine cream cheese, process cheese spread, green onion and mustard in small bowl; mix well.

2. Arrange 3 turkey slices on large sheet of plastic wrap, overlapping slices in center. Spread ¼ of cream cheese mixture evenly onto turkey slices, covering slices completely. Place 1 pretzel at bottom edge of turkey slices; roll up turkey around pretzel. (Be sure to keep all 3 turkey slices together as you roll them around pretzel.)

3. Repeat with remaining ingredients.

makes 4 servings

124

125

quick pizza snacks

3 sandwich-size English muffins, split and toasted

1 can (14½ ounces) Italian-style diced tomatoes, undrained

¾ cup (3 ounces) shredded Italian cheese blend

Bell pepper strips (optional)

Preheat oven to 350°F. Place English muffin halves on ungreased baking sheet. Top each muffin with ¼ cup tomatoes; sprinkle with 2 tablespoons cheese. Bake about 5 minutes or until cheese is melted and lightly browned. Top with pepper strips, if desired.

makes 6 servings

cool sandwich snacks

10 whole graham crackers or chocolate-flavor graham crackers

½ cup chocolate fudge sauce

1 tub (8 ounces) COOL WHIP® Whipped Topping, thawed

Suggested garnishes: Multi-colored sprinkles, assorted candies, finely crushed cookies, chocolate chunks, chopped nuts or toasted BAKER'S® ANGEL FLAKE Coconut

SPREAD ½ of the graham crackers lightly with chocolate sauce. Spread whipped topping about ¾ inch thick on remaining ½ of the graham crackers. Press crackers together lightly, making sandwiches. Roll or lightly press edges in suggested garnish.

FREEZE 4 hours or overnight.   *makes 10 sandwiches*

make ahead: This recipe can be made up to 2 weeks ahead. Wrap well with plastic wrap and freeze.

prep time: 15 minutes
freeze time: 4 hours

126

pleasin' peanutty snack mix

4 cups whole wheat cereal squares *or* **2 cups whole wheat and 2 cups corn or rice cereal squares**

2 cups small pretzel twists or goldfish-shaped pretzels

½ cup dry-roasted peanuts

2 tablespoons creamy peanut butter

1 tablespoon honey

1 tablespoon apple juice or water

2 teaspoons vanilla

Vegetable oil or butter-flavored nonstick cooking spray

½ cup raisins, dried fruit bits or dried cherries (optional)

1. Preheat oven to 250°F.

2. Combine cereal, pretzels and peanuts in large bowl; set aside.

3. Combine peanut butter, honey and apple juice in 1-cup glass measure or small microwavable bowl. Microwave at HIGH 30 seconds or until hot. Stir in vanilla.

4. Drizzle peanut butter mixture evenly over cereal mixture; toss lightly to evenly coat. Place mixture in single layer in ungreased 15×10-inch jelly-roll pan; coat lightly with cooking spray.

5. Bake 8 minutes; stir. Continue baking 8 to 9 minutes or until golden brown. Remove from oven. Add raisins; mix lightly.

6. Spread mixture in single layer on large sheet of foil to cool.

makes 10 (⅔-cup) servings

Snack mixes are the perfect take-along food—just package them in small resealable plastic food storage bags and they're ready to go to any after-school activities or extra-long car trips. And, you can customize any snack mix to your child's tastes: substitute his or her favorite cereal and fruit to make the treat a special one.

128

swimming tuna dip

1 cup low-fat (1%) cottage cheese

1 tablespoon reduced-fat mayonnaise

1 tablespoon lemon juice

2 teaspoons dry ranch-style salad dressing mix

1 can (3 ounces) chunk white tuna packed in water, drained and flaked

2 tablespoons sliced green onion or chopped celery

1 teaspoon dried parsley flakes

1 package (12 ounces) peeled baby carrots

Combine cottage cheese, mayonnaise, lemon juice and salad dressing mix in food processor or blender. Cover and blend until smooth. Stir in tuna, green onion and parsley. Serve with carrots.

makes 4 servings

juicy jell-o®

1 cup boiling water

1 package (4-serving size) JELL-O® Brand Strawberry Flavor Sugar Free Low Calorie Gelatin

1 cup cold orange juice

STIR boiling water into gelatin in medium bowl at least 2 minutes until completely dissolved. Stir in orange juice.

REFRIGERATE 4 hours or until firm.   *makes 4 (½-cup) servings*

prep time: 5 minutes
refrigerate time: 4 hours

make your own pizza shapes

1 package (10 ounces) refrigerated pizza dough

¼ to ½ cup prepared pizza sauce

1 cup shredded mozzarella cheese

1 cup *French's*® *Taste Toppers*™ French Fried Onions

1. Preheat oven to 425°F. Unroll dough onto greased baking sheet. Press or roll dough into 12×8-inch rectangle. With sharp knife or pizza cutter, cut dough into large shape of your choice (butterfly, heart, star). Reroll scraps and cut into mini shapes. (See tip.)

2. Pre-bake crust 7 minutes or until crust just begins to brown. Spread with sauce and top with cheese. Bake 6 minutes or until crust is deep golden brown.

3. Sprinkle with ***Taste Toppers***. Bake 2 minutes longer or until golden.

makes 4 to 6 servings

tip: Pizza dough can be cut with 6-inch shaped cookie cutters. Spread with sauce and top with cheese. Bake about 10 minutes or until crust is golden. Sprinkle with ***Taste Toppers***. Bake 2 minutes longer.

prep time: 10 minutes
cook time: 15 minutes

peanut butter spread

2 tablespoons peanut butter

½ cup part skim ricotta cheese

1 tablespoon brown sugar

¼ teaspoon cinnamon

4 flour tortillas

1 sliced banana or apple, or jam

Mix peanut butter, ricotta cheese brown sugar and cinnamon together. Spread over tortillas and cover with banana, apple or jam. Roll tortillas. Keep extra spread refrigerated.

makes 4 servings

Favorite recipe from **The Sugar Association, Inc.**

soft pretzels

1 package (16 ounces) hot roll mix plus ingredients to prepare mix

1 egg white

2 teaspoons water

2 tablespoons *each* assorted coatings: grated Parmesan cheese, sesame seeds, poppy seeds, dried oregano leaves

1. Prepare hot roll mix according to package directions.

2. Preheat oven to 375°F. Spray baking sheets with nonstick cooking spray; set aside.

3. Divide dough equally into 16 pieces; roll each piece with hands to form a rope, 7 to 10 inches long. Place on prepared cookie sheets; form into desired shape (hearts, wreaths, pretzels, snails, loops, etc.).

4. Beat together egg white and water in small bowl until foamy. Brush onto dough shapes; sprinkle each shape with 1½ teaspoons of one of the coatings.

5. Bake until golden brown, about 15 minutes. Serve warm or at room temperature. *makes 8 servings*

fruit twists: Omit coatings. Prepare dough and roll into ropes as directed. Place ropes on lightly floured surface. Roll out, or pat, each rope into rectangle, ¼ inch thick; brush each rectangle with about 1 teaspoon spreadable fruit or preserves. Fold each rectangle lengthwise in half; twist into desired shape. Bake as directed.

cheese twists: Omit coatings. Prepare dough and roll into ropes as directed. Place ropes on lightly floured surface. Roll out, or pat, each rope into rectangle, ¼ inch thick. Sprinkle each rectangle with about 1 tablespoon shredded Cheddar or other flavor cheese. Fold each rectangle lengthwise in half; twist into desired shape. Bake as directed.

taco popcorn olé

9 cups air-popped popcorn

Butter-flavored cooking spray

1 teaspoon chili powder

½ teaspoon salt

½ teaspoon garlic powder

⅛ teaspoon ground red pepper (optional)

1. Preheat oven to 350°F. Line 15×10-inch jelly-roll pan with foil.

2. Place popcorn in single layer in prepared pan. Coat lightly with cooking spray.

3. Combine chili powder, salt, garlic powder and red pepper in small bowl; sprinkle over popcorn. Mix lightly to coat evenly.

4. Bake 5 minutes or until hot, stirring gently after 3 minutes. Spread mixture in single layer on large sheet of foil to cool.

makes 6 (1½-cup) servings

cook's tip: Store popcorn mixture in tightly covered container at room temperature up to 4 days.

original ranch® snack mix

8 cups Kellogg's® Crispix®* cereal

2½ cups small pretzels

2½ cups bite-size Cheddar cheese crackers (optional)

3 tablespoons vegetable oil

1 packet (1 ounce) HIDDEN VALLEY® Original Ranch® Salad Dressing & Recipe Mix

*Kellogg's® and Crispix® are registered trademarks of Kellogg Company.

Combine cereal, pretzels and crackers in a gallon-size Glad® Zipper Storage Bag. Pour oil over mixture. Seal bag and toss to coat. Add salad dressing & recipe mix; seal bag and toss again until coated.

makes 10 cups

summer fruits with peanut butter-honey dip

⅓ cup smooth or chunky peanut butter

2 tablespoons milk

2 tablespoons honey

1 tablespoon apple juice or water

⅛ teaspoon ground cinnamon

2 cups melon balls, including cantaloupe and honeydew

1 peach or nectarine, pitted and cut into 8 wedges

1 banana, peeled and thickly sliced

1. Place peanut butter in small bowl; gradually stir in milk and honey until blended. Stir in apple juice and cinnamon until mixture is smooth.

2. Serve dip with prepared fruits.

makes 4 servings (about ½ cup dip)

go-with suggestions: Good after a spicy Thai or Asian dinner.

prep time: 20 minutes

banana s'mores

1 firm DOLE® Banana, sliced

12 graham cracker squares

6 large marshmallows

1 bar (1.55 ounces) milk chocolate candy

MICROWAVE DIRECTIONS

• Arrange 4 banana slices on each of 6 graham cracker squares. Top with marshmallow. Microwave on HIGH 12 to 15 seconds or until puffed.

• Place 2 squares chocolate on remaining 6 graham crackers. Microwave on HIGH 1 minute or until just soft. Put halves together to make sandwich. *makes 6 servings*

prep time: 5 minutes
cook time: 1 minute

136

DINNER

octo-dogs and shells

4 hot dogs

1½ cups uncooked small shell pasta

1½ cups frozen mixed vegetables

1 cup prepared Alfredo sauce

Prepared yellow mustard in squeeze bottle

Cheese-flavored fish-shaped crackers

Lay 1 hot dog on side with end facing you. Starting 1 inch from one end of hot dog, slice hot dog vertically in half. Roll hot dog ¼ turn and slice in half vertically again, making 4 segments connected at the top. Slice each segment in half vertically, creating a total of 8 "legs." Repeat with remaining hot dogs.

Place hot dogs in medium saucepan; cover with water. Bring to a boil over medium-high heat. Remove from heat; set aside.

Prepare pasta according to package directions, stirring in vegetables during last 3 minutes of cooking time. Drain; return to pan. Stir in Alfredo sauce. Heat over low heat until heated through. Divide pasta mixture between four plates.

Drain octo-dogs. Arrange one octo-dog on top of pasta mixture on each plate. Draw faces on "heads" of octo-dogs with mustard. Sprinkle crackers over pasta mixture. *makes 4 servings*

ragú® pizza burgers

1 pound ground beef
2 cups RAGÚ® Old World Style® Pasta Sauce
1 cup shredded mozzarella cheese (about 4 ounces)
¼ teaspoon salt
6 English muffins, split and toasted

1. In small bowl, combine ground beef, ½ cup Ragú Pasta Sauce, ½ cup cheese and salt. Shape into 6 patties. Grill or broil until done.

2. Meanwhile, heat remaining pasta sauce. To serve, arrange burgers on muffin halves. Top with remaining cheese, sauce and muffin halves.

makes 6 servings

prep time: 10 minutes
cook time: 15 minutes

school night chicken rice taco toss

1 (6.9-ounce) package RICE-A-RONI® Chicken Flavor
2 tablespoons margarine or butter
1 (16-ounce) jar salsa
1 pound boneless, skinless chicken breasts, chopped
1 cup frozen or canned corn, drained
4 cups shredded lettuce
½ cup (2 ounces) shredded Cheddar cheese
2 cups tortilla chips, coarsely broken
1 medium tomato, chopped

1. In large skillet over medium-high heat, sauté rice-vermicelli mix with margarine until vermicelli is golden brown.

2. Slowly stir in 2 cups water, salsa, chicken and Special Seasonings. Bring to a boil. Reduce heat to low. Cover; simmer 10 minutes.

3. Stir in corn. Cover; simmer 5 to 10 minutes or until rice is tender and chicken is no longer pink inside.

4. Arrange lettuce on large serving platter. Top with chicken-rice mixture. Sprinkle with cheese and tortilla chips. Garnish with tomato.

makes 6 servings

prep time: 10 minutes
cook time: 30 minutes

crunchy fish sticks with rainbow parmesan pasta

⅔ cup milk

2 tablespoons margarine or butter

1 (5.1-ounce) package PASTA RONI® Angel Hair Pasta with Parmesan Cheese

2 cups frozen mixed vegetables or frozen chopped broccoli

Crunchy Fish Sticks (recipe follows)

1. In large saucepan, bring 1⅓ cups water, milk and margarine to a boil.

2. Stir in pasta, vegetables and Special Seasonings; bring back to a boil. Reduce heat to medium. Gently boil uncovered, 4 to 5 minutes or until pasta is tender. Let stand 3 minutes before serving. Serve with Crunchy Fish Sticks or prepared frozen fish sticks.

makes 4 servings

prep time: 20 minutes
cook time: 15 minutes

crunchy fish sticks

3 tablespoons all-purpose flour

½ teaspoon ground black pepper

1 large egg

2 tablespoons milk

3 cups cornflakes, coarsely crushed

1 pound cod fillets, cut into 3×1-inch strips and patted dry

½ to ¾ cup vegetable oil

1. In shallow bowl, combine flour and pepper; set aside. In small bowl, combine egg and milk; set aside. In another shallow bowl, place crushed cornflakes; set aside.

2. Coat fish in flour mixture, dip in egg mixture, then roll in cornflakes, pressing coating gently on each fish strip.

3. In large skillet over medium heat, heat oil. Add fish strips; cook 3 to 4 minutes on each side or until golden brown and fish is cooked through. Drain.

makes 4 servings

barbecue chicken pizza

2 boneless skinless
   chicken breast
   halves (about
   ¾ pound), cut into
   thin strips
1 green pepper, cut into
   strips
¼ cup thinly sliced red
   onion
1 prepared pizza crust
   (12 inch)
⅓ cup BULL'S–EYE®
   Original Barbecue
   Sauce
1 package (8 ounces)
   VELVEETA® Mild
   Cheddar Shredded
   Pasteurized
   Prepared Cheese
   Food

1. Spray large skillet with no stick cooking spray. Add chicken, green pepper and onion; cook and stir on medium-high heat 4 to 5 minutes or until chicken is cooked through.

2. Place crust on cookie sheet. Spread with barbecue sauce. Top with chicken mixture and Velveeta.

3. Bake at 375°F for 12 to 15 minutes or until Velveeta is melted and crust is golden brown.   *makes 4 to 6 servings*

prep time: 15 minutes
bake time: 15 minutes

cheesy broccoli

2 tablespoons CRISCO®
   Oil*
2 cups broccoli
   flowerets
3 tablespoons water
½ teaspoon salt
¼ cup freshly grated
   Parmesan cheese

*Use your favorite Crisco Oil
product.*

1. Heat oil in wok or large skillet on medium-high heat. Add broccoli. Cook and stir 2 minutes.

2. Add water and salt. Cover pan. Steam 3 minutes. Remove broccoli from pan with slotted spoon. Toss with cheese. Serve immediately.
                                                      makes 4 servings

prep time: 5 minutes
total time: 10 minutes

144

145

quick & easy chili

1 pound ground beef

1 cup (1 small) chopped onion

2 cloves garlic, finely chopped

3½ cups (two 15-ounce cans) kidney, pinto or black beans, drained

2½ cups (24-ounce jar) ORTEGA® Thick & Chunky Salsa, hot, medium or mild

½ cup (4-ounce can) ORTEGA® Diced Green Chiles

2 teaspoons chili powder

½ teaspoon dried oregano, crushed

½ teaspoon ground cumin

Topping suggestions: ORTEGA® Thick and Chunky Salsa, shredded Cheddar cheese or Monterey Jack cheese, chopped tomatoes, sliced ripe olives, sliced green onions and sour cream

COOK beef, onion and garlic in large skillet over medium-high heat for 4 to 5 minutes or until beef is no longer pink; drain.

STIR in beans, salsa, chiles, chili powder, oregano and cumin. Bring to a boil. Reduce heat to low; cook, covered, for 20 to 25 minutes.

TOP as desired before serving.   *makes 6 servings*

Why not spend just a few extra minutes in the kitchen and make a double or triple batch of chili? Chili freezes extremely well, and it's always helpful to have a few dinners ready to go at a moment's notice. You can freeze the chili in family-size portions, or freeze it in individual servings in resealable plastic freezer bags—that way the kids can grab a bag and reheat it in the microwave whenever they need to.

tuna mac

2 cups water

2 cups (8 ounces) elbow macaroni, uncooked

¾ pound (12 ounces) VELVEETA® Pasteurized Prepared Cheese Product, cut up

1 package (16 ounces) frozen vegetable blend, thawed, drained

1 can (6 ounces) tuna, drained, flaked

2 tablespoons milk

1. Bring water to boil in saucepan. Stir in macaroni. Reduce heat to medium-low; cover. Simmer 8 to 10 minutes or until macaroni is tender.

2. Add Velveeta, vegetables, tuna and milk; stir until Velveeta is melted. *makes 4 to 6 servings*

a taste of nutrition: With mixed vegetables, Tuna Mac is an excellent source of vitamin A. But you can also substitute any 16-ounce package of a frozen vegetable for the mixed vegetable blend if your family has a particular favorite.

prep time: 10 minutes
cook time: 15 minutes

spicy chicken stromboli

1 cup frozen broccoli florets, thawed

1 can (10 ounces) diced chicken

1½ cups (6 ounces) shredded Monterey Jack cheese with jalapeño peppers

¼ cup chunky salsa

2 green onions, chopped

1 can (10 ounces) refrigerated pizza dough

1. Preheat oven to 400°F. Coarsely chop broccoli. Combine broccoli, chicken, cheese, salsa and green onions in small bowl.

2. Unroll pizza dough. Pat into 15×10-inch rectangle. Sprinkle broccoli mixture evenly over top. Starting with long side, tightly roll into log jelly-roll style. Pinch seam to seal. Place on baking sheet, seam side down.

3. Bake 15 to 20 minutes or until golden brown. Transfer to wire rack to cool slightly. Slice and serve warm. *makes 6 servings*

serving suggestion: Serve with salsa on the side for dipping or pour salsa on top of slices for a boost of added flavor.

prep and cook time: 30 minutes

DINNER

ham & cheese shells & trees

2 tablespoons
    margarine or butter

1 (6.2-ounce) package
    PASTA RONI® Shells
    & White Cheddar

2 cups fresh or frozen
    chopped broccoli

⅔ cup milk

1½ cups ham or cooked
    turkey, cut into thin
    strips (about
    6 ounces)

1. In large saucepan, bring 2 cups water and margarine to a boil.

2. Stir in pasta. Reduce heat to medium. Gently boil uncovered, 6 minutes, stirring occasionally. Stir in broccoli; return to a boil. Boil 6 to 8 minutes or until most of water is absorbed.

3. Stir in milk, ham and Special Seasonings. Return to a boil; boil 1 to 2 minutes or until pasta is tender. Let stand 5 minutes before serving.

makes 4 servings

tip: No leftovers? Ask the deli to slice a ½-inch-thick piece of ham or turkey.

prep time: 5 minutes
cook time: 20 minutes

tuna skillet supper

1 package (8 ounces)
    cream cheese,
    softened

1 cup milk

1 packet (1 ounce)
    HIDDEN VALLEY®
    Original Ranch®
    Salad Dressing &
    Recipe Mix

8 ounces uncooked
    spiral egg noodles

2 cups frozen petite
    peas, thawed

2 cans (6 ounces each)
    tuna or shrimp,
    drained

In a food processor fitted with a metal blade, blend cream cheese, milk and salad dressing & recipe mix until smooth.

Cook pasta according to package directions; drain and combine with peas and tuna in a large skillet. Stir dressing mixture into pasta. Cook over low heat until mixture is hot.   *makes 4 to 6 servings*

148

campfire hot dogs

½ pound ground beef

2 cups RAGÚ® Old World Style® Pasta Sauce

1 can (10¾ to 16 ounces) baked beans

8 frankfurters, cooked

8 frankfurter rolls

1. In 12-inch skillet, brown ground beef over medium-high heat; drain.

2. Stir in Ragú Pasta Sauce and beans. Bring to a boil over high heat. Reduce heat to low and simmer, stirring occasionally, 5 minutes.

3. To serve, arrange frankfurters in rolls and top with sauce mixture. Garnish, if desired, with Cheddar cheese. *makes 8 servings*

tip: For Chili Campfire Hot Dogs, simply stir 2 to 3 teaspoons chili powder into sauce mixture.

prep time: 5 minutes
cook time: 10 minutes

golden mashed potatoes

2½ cups cubed cooked potatoes, mashed

3 tablespoons milk

2 tablespoons butter or margarine

1 tablespoon chopped fresh chives

½ pound (8 ounces) VELVEETA® Pasteurized Prepared Cheese Product, cut up, divided

¼ cup (1 ounce) KRAFT® 100% Grated Parmesan Cheese

1. Beat potatoes, milk, butter and chives until fluffy. Stir in ½ of the Velveeta.

2. Spoon into 1-quart casserole; sprinkle with Parmesan cheese.

3. Bake at 350°F for 20 to 25 minutes or until thoroughly heated. Top with remaining Velveeta. Bake an additional 5 minutes or until Velveeta begins to melt. *makes 4 to 6 servings*

garlic mashed potatoes: Prepare as directed, adding ¾ teaspoon garlic powder or 2 to 3 cloves garlic, minced, with Velveeta. Wait a few minutes before increasing the amount of garlic you add, as garlic flavor will build over time.

prep time: 30 minutes
bake time: 30 minutes

macaroni & cheese boats

1 box (7.25 ounces)
    macaroni & cheese
    mix
¼ cup milk
¼ cup butter
1½ cups shredded
    Cheddar cheese,
    divided
1 tablespoon *French's*®
    Worcestershire
    Sauce
4 red, green or yellow
    bell peppers, halved
    lengthwise
1⅓ cups *French's*® *Taste
    Toppers*™ French
    Fried Onions

1. In medium saucepan, prepare macaroni & cheese as directed on package using ¼ cup milk and ¼ cup butter. Stir in *1 cup* cheese and Worcestershire; set aside.

2. Arrange peppers cut side up in glass baking dish. Add *¼ cup water* to baking dish and cover. Microwave on HIGH 5 minutes or until crisp-tender; drain.

3. Spoon macaroni & cheese into peppers and sprinkle with remaining cheese. Sprinkle with **Taste Toppers** and microwave 2 minutes.

makes 4 servings

prep time: 10 minutes
cook time: 7 minutes

veggie ravioli

2 cans (15 ounces each)
    ravioli
1 bag (16 ounces)
    BIRDS EYE® frozen
    Mixed Vegetables
2 cups shredded
    mozzarella cheese

• In 1½-quart microwave-safe casserole dish, combine ravioli and vegetables.

• Cover; microwave on HIGH 10 minutes, stirring halfway through cook time.

• Uncover; sprinkle with cheese. Microwave 5 minutes more or until cheese is melted.

makes 6 servings

serving suggestion: Sprinkle with grated Parmesan cheese.

prep time: 5 minutes
cook time: 15 minutes

152

ravioli stew

1 tablespoon olive or
   vegetable oil

3 medium carrots,
   chopped

2 medium ribs celery,
   chopped

1 onion, chopped

1 jar (26 to 28 ounces)
   RAGÚ® Hearty
   Robusto!™ Pasta
   Sauce

1 can (14½ ounces)
   chicken broth

1 cup water

1 package (12 to
   16 ounces) fresh or
   frozen mini ravioli,
   cooked and drained

1. In 6-quart saucepot, heat oil over medium-high heat and cook carrots, celery and onion, stirring occasionally, 8 minutes or until golden.

2. Stir in Ragú Pasta Sauce, broth and water. Bring to a boil over high heat. Reduce heat to low and simmer covered 15 minutes.

3. Just before serving, stir in hot ravioli and season, if desired, with salt and ground black pepper. Garnish, if desired, with fresh basil.

makes 6 servings

prep time: 10 minutes
cook time: 30 minutes

herb roasted potatoes

½ cup MIRACLE WHIP®
   or MIRACLE WHIP
   LIGHT® Dressing

1 tablespoon *each* dried
   rosemary, garlic
   powder and onion
   powder

1 teaspoon seasoned
   salt

1 tablespoon water

2 pounds small red
   potatoes, quartered

• **MIX** dressing, seasonings and water in large bowl. Add potatoes; toss to coat. Place potatoes on greased cookie sheet.

• **BAKE** at 400°F for 30 to 40 minutes or until golden brown, stirring after 15 minutes.

makes 8 servings

great substitute: Substitute dried oregano leaves for dried rosemary.

prep time: 15 minutes
bake time: 40 minutes

154

sausage cheeseburger pizza

1 pound **BOB EVANS®** **Original Recipe Roll Sausage**

1 (12-inch) prepared pizza shell

½ cup yellow mustard

2 cups (8 ounces) shredded mozzarella cheese

½ cup chopped onion

15 dill pickle slices

¾ cup (3 ounces) shredded Cheddar cheese

Preheat oven to 425°F. Crumble and cook sausage in medium skillet until browned; drain well on paper towels. Place pizza dough on lightly greased 12-inch pizza pan or baking sheet. Spread mustard over pizza shell; top with mozzarella cheese, sausage and onion. Place pickle slices evenly on top; sprinkle with Cheddar cheese. Bake 12 minutes or until shell is cooked through and cheese is bubbly. Cut into thin wedges or squares and serve hot. Refrigerate leftovers.

makes about 10 appetizer servings

sloppy dogs

1 can (15 ounces) pinto or kidney beans, drained

1 can (14½ ounces) **DEL MONTE®** Zesty Chili Style Chunky Tomatoes

2 fully cooked hot dogs, sliced crosswise

1 teaspoon prepared mustard

4 hamburger buns, split

½ cup shredded Cheddar cheese

MICROWAVE DIRECTIONS

1. Combine all ingredients, except buns and cheese in 2-quart microwavable dish. Cover and microwave on HIGH 6 to 8 minutes or until heated through.

2. Place buns on paper towel; microwave on HIGH 30 seconds to 1 minute. Place buns on 4 dishes, cut side up.

3. Spoon chili over buns. Top with cheese. Serve immediately.

makes 4 servings

prep time: 5 minutes
cook time: 9 minutes

barbecue chicken with cornbread topper

1½ pounds boneless
   skinless chicken
   breasts and thighs

1 can (15 ounces) red
   beans, drained and
   rinsed

1 can (8 ounces) tomato
   sauce

1 cup chopped green
   bell pepper

½ cup barbecue sauce

1 envelope (6.5 ounces)
   cornbread mix

Ingredients for
   cornbread mix

1. Cut chicken into ¾-inch cubes. Heat nonstick skillet over medium heat. Add chicken; cook and stir 5 minutes or until cooked through.

2. Combine chicken, beans, tomato sauce, bell pepper and barbecue sauce in 8-inch microwavable ovenproof dish.

3. Preheat oven to 375°F. Loosely cover chicken mixture with plastic wrap or waxed paper. Microwave on MEDIUM-HIGH (70% power) 8 minutes or until heated through, stirring after 4 minutes.

4. While chicken mixture is heating, prepare cornbread mix according to package directions. Spoon batter over chicken mixture. Bake 15 to 18 minutes or until toothpick inserted in center of cornbread layer comes out clean.   *makes 8 servings*

sweet potato apple bake

3 cups mashed sweet
   potatoes

2 to 3 medium apples,
   peeled, sliced

Ground cinnamon

½ cup apple jelly

Preheat oven to 350°F. Spray 9-inch glass pie plate with nonstick cooking spray. Fill dish evenly with mashed sweet potatoes. Arrange apple slices on top. Sprinkle apples with cinnamon. Melt apple jelly over low heat in small saucepan. Brush over apples. Bake 30 minutes or until apples are tender.   *makes 6 side-dish servings*

Favorite recipe from **New York Apple Association, Inc.**

157

cheesy tacos

1 pound ground beef

¼ cup water

1 package (1¼ ounces) TACO BELL® HOME ORIGINALS™* Taco Seasoning Mix

¾ pound (12 ounces) VELVEETA® Mexican Pasteurized Process Cheese Spread with Jalapeño Peppers, cut up

1 package (4.5 ounces) TACO BELL® HOME ORIGINALS™* Taco Shells or 12 flour tortillas (8 inch)

TACO BELL and HOME ORIGINALS are registered trademarks owned and licensed by Taco Bell Corp.

1. Brown meat in large skillet; drain. Stir in water and taco seasoning mix.

2. Add Velveeta; stir on low heat until Velveeta is melted.

3. Fill heated taco shells with meat mixture. Top with your favorite toppings, such as shredded lettuce, chopped tomato and Taco Bell Home Originals Thick 'N Chunky Salsa. *makes 4 to 6 servings*

serving suggestion: Cheesy Tacos are a fun family dinner. Have your child place the family's favorite taco toppings, such as shredded lettuce and chopped tomato, in a muffin tin to pass around at the table.

prep time: 5 minutes
cook time: 15 minutes

barbecued meat loaf

1 envelope LIPTON® RECIPE SECRETS® Onion Soup Mix

2 pounds ground beef

1½ cups fresh bread crumbs

2 eggs

¾ cup water

⅔ cup barbecue sauce

1. Preheat oven to 350°F. In large bowl, combine all ingredients except ⅓ cup barbecue sauce.

2. In 13×9-inch baking or roasting pan, shape beef mixture into loaf. Top with reserved barbecue sauce.

3. Bake, uncovered, 1 hour or until done. Let stand 10 minutes before serving. *makes 8 servings*

158

159

oven "fried" chicken

2 (4-ounce) boneless skinless chicken breasts, cut in half

4 small (2½ ounces each) skinless chicken drumsticks

1½ cups cornflakes, crushed

1 tablespoon dried parsley flakes

3 tablespoons all-purpose flour

½ teaspoon poultry seasoning

¼ teaspoon garlic salt

¼ teaspoon black pepper

1 egg white

1 tablespoon water

Nonstick cooking spray

1. Preheat oven to 375°F. Rinse chicken. Trim off any fat. Pat dry with paper towels.

2. Mix together cornflake crumbs and parsley in shallow bowl. Combine flour, poultry seasoning, garlic salt and pepper in resealable plastic food storage bag. Whisk together egg white and water in small bowl.

3. Add chicken to flour mixture, one or two pieces at a time. Seal bag; shake until chicken is well coated. Remove chicken from bag, shaking off excess flour. Dip into egg white mixture, coating all sides. Roll in crumb mixture. Place in shallow baking pan. Repeat with remaining chicken, flour mixture, egg white and crumb mixture.

4. Lightly spray chicken pieces with cooking spray. Bake breast pieces 18 to 20 minutes or until no longer pink in center. Bake drumsticks about 25 minutes or until juices run clear. *makes 4 servings*

taco taters

1 pound ground beef

1 jar (26 to 28 ounces) RAGÚ® Old World Style® Pasta Sauce

1 package (1.25 ounces) taco seasoning mix

6 large all-purpose potatoes, unpeeled and baked

1. In 12-inch skillet, brown ground beef over medium-high heat; drain. Stir in Ragú Pasta Sauce and taco seasoning mix and cook 5 minutes.

2. To serve, cut a lengthwise slice from top of each potato. Evenly spoon beef mixture onto each potato. Garnish, if desired, with shredded Cheddar cheese and sour cream. *makes 6 servings*

prep time: 5 minutes
cook time: 15 minutes

160

creamy mashed potato bake

3 cups mashed
    potatoes

1 cup sour cream

¼ cup milk

¼ teaspoon garlic
    powder

1⅓ cups *French's® Taste
    Toppers™* French
    Fried Onions,
    divided

1 cup (4 ounces)
    shredded Cheddar
    cheese, divided

1. Preheat oven to 350°F. Combine mashed potatoes, sour cream, milk and garlic powder.

2. Spoon half of mixture into 2-quart casserole. Sprinkle with ⅔ *cup* **Taste Toppers** and ½ *cup* cheese. Top with remaining potato mixture.

3. Bake 30 minutes or until hot. Top with remaining ⅔ *cup* **Taste Toppers** and ½ *cup* cheese. Bake 5 minutes or until **Taste Toppers** are golden.   *makes 6 servings*

prep time: 5 minutes
cook time: 35 minutes

philly cheese steak sandwich

1 onion, sliced

1 green bell pepper, cut
    into thin strips

2 tablespoons butter or
    margarine

2 packages (6 ounces
    each) HILLSHIRE
    FARM® Deli Select
    Roast Beef, cut into
    thin strips

4 submarine or hoagie
    rolls, cut into halves

½ pound provolone
    cheese, sliced

Sauté onion and bell pepper in butter in medium saucepan over medium-high heat until onion is transparent. Mix in Roast Beef; heat until beef is warm. Evenly divide beef mixture into 4 portions; fill each roll with beef mixture. Top each sandwich evenly with cheese.

makes 4 servings

162

hot dog macaroni

- 1 package (8 ounces) hot dogs
- 1 cup uncooked corkscrew pasta
- 1 cup shredded Cheddar cheese
- 1 box (10 ounces) BIRDS EYE® frozen Green Peas
- 1 cup 1% milk

- Slice hot dogs into bite-size pieces; set aside.

- In large saucepan, cook pasta according to package directions; drain and return to saucepan.

- Stir in hot dogs, cheese, peas and milk. Cook over medium heat 10 minutes or until cheese is melted, stirring occasionally.

makes 4 servings

prep time: 10 minutes
cook time: 20 minutes

pasta pronto

- 8 ounces linguine or spaghetti, uncooked
- 1 pound ground beef, ground turkey or mild Italian sausage
- 1 cup coarsely chopped onions
- 1 clove garlic, minced
- 2 cans (14½ ounces each) DEL MONTE® Pasta Style Chunky Tomatoes, undrained
- 1 can (8 ounces) DEL MONTE® Tomato Sauce
- About ¼ cup (1 ounce) grated Parmesan cheese

1. Cook pasta according to package directions; drain and keep hot.

2. In large skillet, brown meat with onions and garlic; drain.

3. Add tomatoes and tomato sauce. Cook, stirring frequently, 15 minutes.

4. Spoon sauce over hot pasta; sprinkle with cheese. Serve with French bread, if desired.

makes 4 servings

prep time: 10 minutes
cook time: 20 minutes

saucy chicken & vegetables

6 boneless skinless chicken breast halves

1 can (10¾ ounces) condensed cream of chicken soup

1⅓ cups *French's*® Taste Toppers™ French Fried Onions, divided

1 cup milk or water

½ cup grated Parmesan cheese

3 cups bite-size vegetables*

2 teaspoons dried basil leaves

Try these variations: 3 cups cut-up tomatoes, zucchini and asparagus; 3 cups cut-up broccoli and carrots; 1 (16-ounce) package frozen vegetable combination, thawed.

1. Heat *1 tablespoon oil* in 12-inch nonstick skillet until hot. Cook chicken 10 minutes or until thoroughly browned on both sides. Remove; set aside.

2. In same skillet, combine soup, ⅔ *cup* **Taste Toppers**, milk and cheese. Heat to boiling. Stir in vegetables and basil. Return chicken to skillet. Reduce heat to medium-low. Cook 5 minutes or until chicken is no longer pink in center, stirring occasionally.

3. Top with remaining ⅔ *cup* **Taste Toppers**. Serve with hot cooked rice or pasta, if desired. *makes 6 servings*

tip: For a crispier onion topping, microwave **French's**® Taste Toppers™ 1 minute on HIGH.

prep time: 10 minutes
cook time: 20 minutes

cheddar burger mashed potato bake

2 pounds ground beef

1 medium onion, chopped

1 jar (16 ounces) RAGÚ® Cheese Creations!® Double Cheddar Sauce

2 teaspoons dry mustard

4 cups prepared mashed potatoes

Preheat oven to 425°F. In 12-inch skillet, brown ground beef over medium-high heat; drain. Add onion and cook, stirring occasionally, 2 minutes. Stir in Ragú Cheese Creations! Sauce, mustard and, if desired, salt and ground black pepper to taste. Simmer uncovered, stirring occasionally, 3 minutes or until heated through.

Turn into 2-quart casserole; evenly top with mashed potatoes. Bake 25 minutes or until potatoes are lightly golden. *makes 8 servings*

recipe tip: When making mashed potatoes, use Idaho or all-purpose potatoes for marvelous flavor and texture. Heat the milk before adding it—this minimizes any starchiness.

bbq chicken wrap sandwiches

1 tablespoon oil

1 pound boneless
skinless chicken
breast, cut into thin
strips

2 medium green *or* red
peppers, sliced

1 medium onion, sliced

1 cup KRAFT® Original
Barbecue Sauce

4 flour tortillas
(10 inches) *or*
8 flour tortillas
(6 inches)

HEAT oil in large skillet on medium-high heat. Add chicken; cook and stir 8 minutes or until chicken is cooked through.

ADD green peppers, onion and barbecue sauce; cover. Cook until vegetables are tender, stirring occasionally. Divide chicken mixture among tortillas; roll up.   *makes 4 servings*

variation: Serve barbecue chicken mixture over rice for another great dinner.

prep time: 10 minutes
cook time: 12 minutes

pizza casserole

1 pound BOB EVANS®
Italian Roll Sausage

12 ounces wide noodles,
cooked according to
package directions

2 (14-ounce) jars
pepperoni pizza
sauce

2 cups (8 ounces)
shredded Cheddar
cheese

2 cups (8 ounces)
shredded
mozzarella cheese

6 ounces sliced
pepperoni

Preheat oven to 350°F. Crumble and cook sausage in medium skillet over medium heat until browned. Drain on paper towels. Layer half of noodles in lightly greased 13×9-inch casserole dish. Top with half of sausage, half of pizza sauce, half of cheeses and half of pepperoni. Repeat layers with remaining ingredients, reserving several pepperoni slices for garnish on top of casserole. Bake 35 to 40 minutes. Refrigerate leftovers.   *makes 6 to 8 servings*

skillet franks and potatoes

3 tablespoons vegetable oil, divided

4 HEBREW NATIONAL® Quarter Pound Dinner Beef Franks or 4 Beef Knockwurst

3 cups chopped cooked red potatoes

1 cup chopped onion

1 cup chopped seeded green bell pepper or combination of green and red bell peppers

3 tablespoons chopped fresh parsley (optional)

1 teaspoon dried sage leaves

½ teaspoon salt

¼ teaspoon freshly ground black pepper

Heat 1 tablespoon oil in large nonstick skillet over medium heat. Score franks; add to skillet. Cook franks until browned. Transfer to plate; set aside.

Add remaining 2 tablespoons oil to skillet. Add potatoes, onion and bell pepper; cook and stir about 12 to 14 minutes or until potatoes are golden brown. Stir in parsley, sage, salt and pepper.

Return franks to skillet; push down into potato mixture. Cook about 5 minutes or until heated through, turning once halfway through cooking time.

makes 4 servings

Round red potatoes, also called boiling potatoes, have a waxy flesh; they contain more moisture and less starch than russet potatoes which makes them better suited for boiling. Leaving the peel on the potatoes adds extra flavor and nutrients (as well as color) to the dish; just scrub them well with a vegetable brush before cooking.

cheeseburger mac

1 pound ground beef

2¾ cups water

⅓ cup catsup

1 to 2 teaspoons onion powder

2 cups (8 ounces) elbow macaroni, uncooked

¾ pound (12 ounces) VELVEETA® Pasteurized Prepared Cheese Product, cut up

1. Brown meat in large skillet; drain.

2. Stir in water, catsup and onion powder. Bring to boil. Stir in macaroni. Reduce heat to medium-low; cover. Simmer 8 to 10 minutes or until macaroni is tender.

3. Add Velveeta; stir until melted.

makes 4 to 6 servings

safe food handling: Store ground beef in the coldest part of the refrigerator for up to 2 days. Make sure raw juices do not touch other foods. Ground meat can be wrapped airtight and frozen for up to 3 months.

prep time: 10 minutes
cook time: 15 minutes

french bread pizza

½ pound bulk Italian turkey sausage

½ pound extra lean ground beef

1 (15½-ounce) can HUNT'S® Manwich Sloppy Joe Sauce

2 tablespoons grated Parmesan cheese

1 teaspoon dried oregano

1 (16-ounce) loaf unsliced French bread

1 cup shredded fat-free mozzarella cheese

1. In large skillet, brown sausage with beef; drain. Stir in Manwich Sauce, Parmesan cheese and oregano. Simmer, uncovered, for 5 minutes.

2. Halve bread lengthwise. Top *each* half loaf with *half* of meat mixture and mozzarella cheese.

3. Place on baking sheet and broil 5 to 6 inches from heat source for 3 minutes or until hot and bubbly. Cut into 16 slices.

makes 16 servings

mini chicken pot pies

1 container (about 16 ounces) refrigerated reduced-fat buttermilk biscuits

1½ cups milk

1 package (1.8 ounces) white sauce mix

2 cups cut-up cooked chicken

1 cup frozen assorted vegetables, partially thawed

2 cups shredded Cheddar cheese

2 cups *French's® Taste Toppers™* French Fried Onions

1. Preheat oven to 400°F. Separate biscuits; press into 8 (8-ounce) custard cups, pressing up sides to form crust.

2. Whisk milk and sauce mix in medium saucepan. Bring to boiling over medium-high heat. Reduce heat to medium-low; simmer 1 minute, whisking constantly, until thickened. Stir in chicken and vegetables.

3. Spoon about ⅓ cup chicken mixture into each crust. Place cups on baking sheet. Bake 15 minutes or until golden brown. Top each with cheese and *Taste Toppers*. Bake 3 minutes or until golden. To serve, remove from cups and transfer to serving plates.   *makes 8 servings*

prep time: 15 minutes
cook time: about 20 minutes

groovy angel hair goulash

1 pound lean ground beef

2 tablespoons margarine or butter

1 (4.8-ounce) package PASTA RONI® Angel Hair Pasta with Herbs

1 (14½-ounce) can diced tomatoes, undrained

1 cup frozen or canned corn, drained

1. In large skillet over medium-high heat, brown ground beef. Remove from skillet; drain. Set aside.

2. In same skillet, bring 1½ cups water and margarine to a boil.

3. Stir in pasta; cook 1 minute or just until pasta softens slightly. Stir in tomatoes, corn, beef and Special Seasonings; return to a boil. Reduce heat to medium. Gently boil uncovered, 4 to 5 minutes or until pasta is tender, stirring frequently. Let stand 3 to 5 minutes before serving.

makes 4 servings

prep time: 5 minutes
cook time: 15 minutes

ranch crispy chicken

¼ **cup unseasoned dry bread crumbs or cornflake crumbs**

1 **packet (1 ounce) HIDDEN VALLEY® Original Ranch® Salad Dressing & Recipe Mix**

6 **bone-in chicken pieces**

Combine bread crumbs and salad dressing & recipe mix in a gallon-size Glad® Zipper Storage Bag. Add chicken pieces; seal bag. Shake to coat chicken. Bake chicken on ungreased baking pan at 375°F. for 50 minutes or until no longer pink in center and juices run clear.

makes 4 to 6 servings

ham and potato au gratin

3 **tablespoons butter or margarine**

3 **tablespoons all-purpose flour**

2 **cups milk**

1½ **cups (6 ounces) shredded Cheddar cheese**

1 **tablespoon Dijon mustard**

2 **cups HILLSHIRE FARM® Lean & Hearty Ham cut into thin strips**

1 **package (24 ounces) frozen shredded hash brown potatoes, thawed**

1 **package (10 ounces) frozen chopped spinach, thawed and drained**

Preheat oven to 350°F.

Melt butter in large saucepan over medium heat; stir in flour. Add milk. Cook and stir until bubbly; cook 1 minute more. Remove from heat. Stir in cheese and mustard; set aside.

Place ½ of Ham into ungreased medium casserole. Top ham with ½ of potatoes and ½ of milk mixture. Spoon spinach over top. Repeat layers with remaining ham, potatoes and milk mixture.

Bake, uncovered, 30 minutes or until heated through.

makes 8 servings

174

stuffed franks 'n' taters

4 cups frozen hash
    brown potatoes,
    thawed
1 can (10¾ ounces)
    condensed cream
    of celery soup
1⅓ cups *French's®* *Taste*
    Toppers™ French
    Fried Onions,
    divided
1 cup (4 ounces)
    shredded Cheddar
    cheese, divided
1 cup sour cream
½ teaspoon salt
¼ teaspoon pepper
6 frankfurters

Preheat oven to 400°F. In large bowl, combine potatoes, soup, ⅔ cup **Taste Toppers**, ½ cup cheese, sour cream and seasonings. Spread potato mixture in 12×8-inch baking dish. Split frankfurters lengthwise almost into halves. Arrange frankfurters, split-side up, along center of casserole. Bake, covered, at 400°F for 30 minutes or until heated through. Fill frankfurters with remaining cheese and ⅔ cup **Taste Toppers**; bake, uncovered, 1 to 3 minutes or until **Taste Toppers** are golden brown. *makes 6 servings*

microwave directions: Prepare potato mixture as above; spread in 12×8-inch microwave-safe dish. Cook, covered, on HIGH 8 minutes; stir potato mixture halfway through cooking time. Split frankfurters and arrange on potatoes as above. Cook, covered, 4 to 6 minutes or until frankfurters are heated through. Rotate dish halfway through cooking time. Fill frankfurters with remaining cheese and ⅔ cup onions; cook, uncovered, 1 minute or until cheese melts. Let stand 5 minutes.

cinnamon apple rings

3 large cooking apples
¼ cup lemon juice
1 cup water
½ cup sugar
¼ cup red cinnamon
    candies

Peel and core apples; cut crosswise into ½-inch-thick rings. Toss with lemon juice to prevent discoloration. Combine water, sugar and candies in large saucepan. Bring to a boil, stirring until sugar and candies are dissolved. Add apple rings and simmer until just tender, about 15 minutes. Let cool in liquid. Drain. *makes 4 servings*

Favorite recipe from **Perdue Farms Incorporated**

nifty nacho dinner

8 ounces lean ground beef

1 (6.8-ounce) package RICE-A-RONI® Beef Flavor

2 tablespoons margarine or butter

1 (16-ounce) can refried beans

1 (11-ounce) can Mexican-style corn or sweet corn, drained

1½ cups (6 ounces) shredded Cheddar cheese, divided

Tortilla chips

1. In large skillet over medium-high heat, brown ground beef. Remove from skillet; drain. Set aside.

2. In same skillet over medium heat, sauté rice-vermicelli mix with margarine until vermicelli is golden brown.

3. Slowly stir in 2½ cups water and Special Seasonings; bring to a boil. Reduce heat to low. Cover; simmer 10 minutes.

4. Stir in refried beans, corn, 1 cup cheese and beef; return to a simmer. Cover; simmer 5 to 10 minutes or until rice is tender. Top with remaining ½ cup cheese. Serve in skillet with tortilla chips.

makes 6 servings

prep time: 5 minutes
cook time: 30 minutes

taco cups

1 pound ground beef OR pork

1 package (1.0 ounce) LAWRY'S® Taco Spices & Seasonings

1¼ cups water

¼ cup mild salsa

2 packages (8 ounces each) refrigerator biscuits

½ cup (2 ounces) shredded cheddar cheese

In medium skillet, cook ground beef over medium-high heat until crumbly; drain fat. Add Taco Spices & Seasonings and water; mix well. Bring to a boil over medium-high heat; reduce heat to low and simmer, uncovered, 10 minutes. Stir in salsa. Separate biscuits and press each biscuit into an ungreased muffin cup. Spoon equal amounts of meat mixture into each muffin cup; sprinkle each with cheese. Bake, uncovered, in 350°F oven 12 minutes. *makes 12 pastries*

serving suggestion: Serve as a snack or a main dish.

hint: Flatten any leftover biscuit dough into disks; sprinkle with cinnamon-sugar mixture and bake in 350°F oven until golden.

177

twice baked ranch potatoes

4 baking potatoes

½ cup KRAFT® Ranch Dressing

¼ cup BREAKSTONE'S® or KNUDSEN® Sour Cream

1 tablespoon OSCAR MAYER® Real Bacon Bits

¼ pound (4 ounces) VELVEETA® Pasteurized Prepared Cheese Product, cut up

1. Bake potatoes at 400°F for 1 hour. Slice off tops of potatoes; scoop out centers, leaving ⅛-inch shell.

2. Mash potatoes. Add dressing, sour cream and bacon bits; beat until fluffy. Stir Velveeta into potato mixture. Spoon into shells.

3. Bake at 350°F for 20 minutes. *makes 4 servings*

how to bake potatoes: Russet potatoes are best for baking. Scrub potatoes well, blot dry and rub the skin with a little oil and salt. Prick the skin of the potatoes with a fork so steam can escape. Stand them on end in a muffin tin. Bake at 400°F for 60 minutes or until tender.

prep time: 20 minutes plus baking potatoes
bake time: 20 minutes

corny sloppy joes

1 pound lean ground beef or ground turkey

1 small onion, chopped

1 can (15½ ounces) sloppy joe sauce

1 box (10 ounces) BIRDS EYE® frozen Sweet Corn

6 hamburger buns

• In large skillet, cook beef and onion over high heat until beef is well browned.

• Stir in sloppy joe sauce and corn; reduce heat to low and simmer 5 minutes or until heated through.

• Serve mixture in hamburger buns. *makes 6 servings*

serving suggestion: Sprinkle with shredded Cheddar cheese.

prep time: 5 minutes
cook time: 15 minutes

kid's choice meatballs

1½ pounds ground beef
¼ cup dry seasoned bread crumbs
¼ cup grated Parmesan cheese
3 tablespoons *French's®* Worcestershire Sauce
1 egg
2 jars (14 ounces *each*) spaghetti sauce

1. Preheat oven to 425°F. In bowl, gently mix beef, bread crumbs, cheese, Worcestershire and egg. Shape into 1-inch meatballs. Place on rack in roasting pan. Bake 15 minutes or until cooked.

2. In large saucepan, combine meatballs and spaghetti sauce. Cook until heated through. Serve over cooked pasta.

makes 6 to 8 servings (about 48 meatballs)

quick meatball tip: On waxed paper, pat meat mixture into 8×6×1-inch rectangle. With knife, cut crosswise and lengthwise into 1-inch rows. Roll each small square into a ball.

prep time: 10 minutes
cook time: 20 minutes

bbq beef pizza

½ pound lean ground beef
⅔ cup prepared barbecue sauce
1 medium green bell pepper
1 (14-inch) prepared pizza crust
3 to 4 onion slices, rings separated
½ (2¼-ounce) can sliced black olives, drained
1 cup (4 ounces) shredded cheese (Colby and Monterey Jack mix)

1. Preheat oven to 400°F. Place meat in large skillet; cook over high heat 6 to 8 minutes or until meat is no longer pink, breaking meat apart with wooden spoon. Pour off drippings; remove from heat. Stir in barbecue sauce.

2. While meat is cooking, seed bell pepper and slice into ¼-inch-thick rings. Place pizza crust on baking pan. Spread meat mixture over pizza crust to within ½ inch of edge. Arrange onion slices and pepper rings over meat. Sprinkle with olives and cheese. Bake 8 minutes or until cheese is melted. Cut into 8 wedges.   *makes 3 to 4 servings*

prep and cook time: 20 minutes

golden chicken nuggets

1 pound boneless skinless chicken breasts, cut into 1½-inch pieces

¼ cup *French's®* Honey Mustard

2 cups *French's® Taste Toppers™* French Fried Onions, finely crushed

1. Preheat oven to 400°F. Toss chicken with mustard in medium bowl.

2. Place *Taste Toppers* into resealable plastic food storage bag. Toss chicken in *Taste Toppers*, a few pieces at a time, pressing gently to adhere.

3. Place chicken in shallow baking pan. Bake 15 minutes or until chicken is no longer pink in center. Serve with additional honey mustard.

makes 4 servings

prep time: 5 minutes
cook time: 15 minutes

baked pasta and cheese supreme

8 ounces uncooked fusilli pasta

8 ounces uncooked bacon, diced

½ onion, chopped

2 cloves garlic, minced

2 teaspoons dried oregano, divided

1 can (8 ounces) tomato sauce

1 teaspoon hot pepper sauce (optional)

1½ cups (6 ounces) shredded Cheddar or Colby cheese

½ cup fresh bread crumbs (from 1 slice of white bread)

1 tablespoon melted butter

Preheat oven to 400°F. Cook pasta according to package directions; drain. Meanwhile, cook bacon in large ovenproof skillet over medium heat until crisp; drain.

Add onion, garlic and 1 teaspoon oregano to skillet; cook and stir about 3 minutes or until onion is tender. Stir in tomato sauce and hot pepper sauce. Add cooked pasta and cheese to skillet; stir to coat.

Combine bread crumbs, remaining 1 teaspoon oregano and melted butter in small bowl; sprinkle over pasta mixture. Bake about 5 minutes or until hot and bubbly. Garnish, if desired.

makes 4 servings

tuna quesadilla stack

4 (10-inch) flour
tortillas, divided

¼ cup plus
2 tablespoons pinto
or black bean dip

1 can (9 ounces) tuna
packed in water,
drained and flaked

2 cups (8 ounces)
shredded Cheddar
cheese

1 can (14½ ounces)
diced tomatoes,
drained

½ cup thinly sliced
green onions

½ tablespoon butter or
margarine, melted

1. Preheat oven to 400°F.

2. Place 1 tortilla on 12-inch pizza pan. Spread with 2 tablespoons bean dip, leaving ½-inch border. Top with one third each of tuna, cheese, tomatoes and green onions. Repeat layers twice beginning with tortilla and ending with onions.

3. Top with remaining tortilla, pressing gently. Brush with melted butter.

4. Bake 15 minutes or until cheese melts and top is lightly browned. Cool and cut into 8 wedges. *makes 4 servings*

tip: For a special touch, serve with assorted toppings, such as guacamole, sour cream and salsa.

prep and cook time: 25 minutes

creamy broccoli and cheese

1 package (8 ounces)
cream cheese,
softened

¾ cup milk

1 packet (1 ounce)
HIDDEN VALLEY®
Original Ranch®
Salad Dressing &
Recipe Mix

1 pound fresh broccoli,
cooked and drained

½ cup (2 ounces)
shredded sharp
Cheddar cheese

In a food processor fitted with a metal blade, blend cream cheese, milk and salad dressing & recipe mix until smooth. Pour over broccoli in a 9-inch baking dish; stir well. Top with cheese. Bake at 350°F for 25 minutes or until cheese is melted. *makes 4 servings*

ham & barbecued bean skillet

1 tablespoon vegetable oil

1 cup chopped onion

1 teaspoon minced garlic

1 can (15 ounces) red or pink kidney beans, rinsed and drained

1 can (15 ounces) cannellini or Great Northern beans, rinsed and drained

1 cup chopped green bell pepper

½ cup firmly packed light brown sugar

½ cup catsup

2 tablespoons cider vinegar

2 teaspoons dry mustard

1 fully cooked smoked ham steak (about 12 ounces), cut ½ inch thick

1. Heat oil in large deep skillet over medium-high heat until hot. Add onion and garlic; cook 3 minutes, stirring occasionally.

2. Add kidney beans, cannellini beans, bell pepper, brown sugar, catsup, vinegar and mustard; mix well.

3. Trim fat from ham; cut into ½-inch pieces. Add ham to bean mixture; simmer over medium heat 5 minutes or until sauce thickens and mixture is heated through, stirring occasionally. *makes 4 servings*

serving suggestion: Serve with a Caesar salad and crisp breadsticks.

prep and cook time: 20 minutes

If you're using a garlic press to mince garlic, you don't need to peel the cloves before putting them through the press. When you squeeze a clove in the press, the garlic flesh will be forced through the holes while the skin stays behind in the press. (This also makes it easier to clean the press.)

pizza soup

- 2 cans (10¾ ounces each) condensed tomato soup
- ¾ teaspoon garlic powder
- ½ teaspoon dried oregano leaves
- ¾ cup uncooked tiny pasta shells (¼-inch)
- 1 cup shredded quick-melting mozzarella cheese
- 1 cup *French's® Taste Toppers™* French Fried Onions

1. Combine soup, *2 soup cans of water,* garlic powder and oregano in small saucepan. Bring to boiling over medium-high heat.

2. Add pasta. Cook 8 minutes or until pasta is tender.

3. Stir in cheese. Cook until cheese melts. Sprinkle with *Taste Toppers*.

makes 4 servings

prep time: 5 minutes
cook time: 10 minutes

original ortega® taco recipe

- 1 pound ground beef
- ¾ cup water
- 1 package (1¼ ounces) ORTEGA® Taco Seasoning Mix
- 1 package (12) ORTEGA® Taco Shells, warmed
- Toppings: shredded lettuce, chopped tomatoes, shredded mild Cheddar cheese, ORTEGA® Thick & Smooth Taco Sauce

BROWN beef; drain, Stir in water and seasoning mix. Bring to a boil. Reduce heat to low; cook, stirring occasionally, for 5 to 6 minutes or until mixture is thickened.

FILL taco shells with beef mixture. Top with lettuce, tomatoes, cheese and taco sauce.

makes 6 servings

salsa macaroni & cheese

1 jar (16 ounces) RAGÚ®
    Cheese Creations!®
    Double Cheddar
    Sauce

1 cup prepared mild
    salsa

8 ounces elbow
    macaroni, cooked
    and drained

1. In 2-quart saucepan, heat Ragú Cheese Creations! Sauce over medium heat. Stir in salsa; heat through.

2. Toss with hot macaroni. Serve immediately.   *makes 4 servings*

prep time: 5 minutes
cook time: 15 minutes

skillet chicken enchiladas

1 pound boneless
    skinless chicken
    breasts, cut into
    1-inch pieces

½ pound (8 ounces)
    VELVEETA®
    Pasteurized
    Prepared Cheese
    Product, cut up

½ cup TACO BELL®
    HOME
    ORIGINALS™* Thick
    'N Chunky Salsa

1 teaspoon chili powder

1 teaspoon ground
    cumin (optional)

10 flour tortillas (6 inch)

TACO BELL and HOME ORIGINALS are registered trademarks owned and licensed by Taco Bell Corp.

1. Spray large skillet with no stick cooking spray. Add chicken; cook and stir on medium-high heat 3 to 4 minutes or until cooked through. Reduce heat to medium-low.

2. Add Velveeta, salsa and seasonings. Cook and stir 1 minute or until Velveeta is completely melted.

3. Spoon ¼ cup chicken mixture in center of each tortilla; roll up. Arrange on serving dish. Serve immediately with shredded lettuce, chopped tomato, BREAKSTONE'S® or KNUDSEN® Sour Cream and additional salsa, if desired.   *makes 5 servings*

prep time: 10 minutes
cook time: 10 minutes

oven "fries"

2 small baking potatoes (10 ounces)

2 teaspoons olive oil

¼ teaspoon salt or onion salt

1. Preheat oven to 450°F. Peel potatoes and cut lengthwise into ¼-inch strips. Place in colander; rinse under cold running water and drain well. Pat dry with paper towels. Place potatoes in small resealable plastic food storage bag. Drizzle with oil. Seal bag; shake to coat potatoes with oil.

2. Arrange potatoes in single layer on baking sheet. Bake 20 to 25 minutes or until light brown and crisp. Sprinkle with salt or onion salt.

makes 2 servings

stromboli

1 package (10 ounces) refrigerated pizza dough

⅓ cup *French's*® Deli Brown Mustard

¾ pound sliced deli meats and cheese such as salami, provolone cheese and ham

1 egg, beaten

1 teaspoon poppy or sesame seeds

1. Preheat oven to 425°F. Unroll pizza dough on lightly floured board. Roll into 13×10-inch rectangle. Spread mustard evenly on dough. Layer luncheon meats and cheeses on dough, overlapping slices, leaving a 1-inch border around edges.

2. Fold one-third of dough toward center from long edge of rectangle. Fold second side toward center enclosing filling. Pinch long edge to seal. Pinch ends together and tuck under dough. Place on greased baking sheet.

3. Cut shallow crosswise slits on top of dough, spacing 3 inches apart. Brush stromboli lightly with beaten egg; sprinkle with poppy seeds. Bake 15 to 18 minutes or until deep golden brown. Remove to rack; cool slightly. Serve warm.

makes 12 servings

prep time: 20 minutes
cook time: 15 minutes

190

hot dog burritos

1 can (16 ounces) pork and beans

⅓ cup ketchup

2 tablespoons *French's*® Classic Yellow® Mustard

2 tablespoons brown sugar

8 frankfurters, cooked

8 (8-inch) flour tortillas, heated

1. Combine beans, ketchup, mustard and brown sugar in medium saucepan. Bring to boiling over medium-high heat. Reduce heat to low and simmer 2 minutes.

2. Arrange frankfurters in heated tortillas and top with bean mixture. Roll up jelly-roll style.   *makes 8 servings*

tip: Try topping dogs with ***French's*® Taste Toppers**™ before rolling up!

prep time: 5 minutes
cook time: 8 minutes

tamale pie

1 tablespoon olive or vegetable oil

1 small onion, chopped

1 pound ground beef

1 envelope LIPTON® RECIPE SECRETS® Onion Soup Mix*

1 can (14½ ounces) stewed tomatoes, undrained

½ cup water

1 can (15 to 19 ounces) red kidney beans, rinsed and drained

1 package (8½ ounces) corn muffin mix

• Preheat oven to 400°F.

• In 12-inch skillet, heat oil over medium heat and cook onion, stirring occasionally, 3 minutes or until tender. Stir in ground beef and cook until browned.

• Stir in onion soup mix blended with tomatoes and water. Bring to a boil over high heat, stirring with spoon to crush tomatoes. Reduce heat to low and stir in beans. Simmer uncovered, stirring occasionally, 10 minutes. Turn into 2-quart casserole.

• Prepare corn muffin mix according to package directions. Spoon evenly over casserole.

• Bake uncovered 15 minutes or until corn topping is golden and filling is hot.   *makes about 6 servings*

*Also terrific with LIPTON® RECIPE SECRETS® Fiesta Herb with Red Pepper, Onion-Mushroom, Beefy Onion or Beefy Mushroom Soup Mix.

192

193

original ranch® roasted potatoes

2 pounds small red potatoes, quartered

¼ cup vegetable oil

1 packet (1 ounce) HIDDEN VALLEY® Original Ranch® Salad Dressing & Recipe Mix

Place potatoes in a gallon-size Glad® Zipper Storage Bag. Pour oil over potatoes. Seal bag and toss to coat. Add salad dressing & recipe mix; seal bag and toss again until coated. Bake in ungreased baking pan at 450°F for 30 to 35 minutes or until potatoes are brown and crisp.

makes 4 to 6 servings

tuna supper sandwiches

2 cups shredded Cheddar cheese

⅓ cup chopped green onions, including tops

⅓ cup chopped red bell pepper

1 can (2¼ ounces) sliced ripe olives, drained

2 tablespoons minced fresh parsley

1 teaspoon curry powder

Seasoned salt to taste

1 can (12 ounces) STARKIST® Solid White or Chunk Light Tuna, drained and chunked

½ cup light mayonnaise

6 soft French rolls (7 inches *each*), halved lengthwise

In medium bowl, place cheese, onions, red pepper, olives, parsley, curry powder and salt; mix lightly. Add tuna and mayonnaise; toss lightly with fork. Cover baking sheet with foil; place rolls on foil. Spread about ⅓ cup mixture on each half. Bake in 450°F oven 10 to 12 minutes or until tops are bubbling and beginning to brown. Cool slightly before serving.

makes 12 servings

prep time: 18 minutes
cook time: 12 minutes

original ranch® roasted potatoes

santa fe chicken & pasta

1 jar (12 ounces) mild chunky salsa

1 can (10¾ ounces) condensed Cheddar cheese soup

¾ cup sour cream

5 cups hot cooked ziti pasta (8 ounces uncooked)

1⅓ cups *French's®* *Taste Toppers™* French Fried Onions, divided

1 package (10 ounces) fully cooked carved chicken breast (2 cups cut-up chicken)

1 cup (4 ounces) cubed Monterey Jack cheese with jalapeño

1. Preheat oven to 375°F. In large bowl, mix salsa, soup and sour cream. Stir in pasta, ⅔ cup **Taste Toppers**, chicken and cheese; mix well. Spoon into 3-quart casserole.

2. Cover; bake 40 minutes or until hot and bubbly. Stir.

3. Sprinkle with remaining ⅔ *cup* **Taste Toppers**. Bake 3 minutes or until **Taste Toppers** are golden. *makes 8 servings*

prep time: 10 minutes
cook time: 43 minutes

When cooking pasta for a casserole, don't cook it as long as the package recommends. Reduce the cooking time by about one-third, as the pasta will continue to cook and absorb liquid when the casserole goes in the oven.

minestrone soup with mini meatballs

1 pound ground beef or ground turkey

1 teaspoon dried Italian seasoning

½ teaspoon garlic powder, divided

2 tablespoons vegetable oil, divided

5 cups assorted fresh vegetables*

1 envelope LIPTON® RECIPE SECRETS® Onion Soup Mix

4 cups water

1 can (28 ounces) Italian plum tomatoes, undrained

1 teaspoon sugar

Use any of the following to equal 5 cups: green beans, cut into 1-inch pieces; diced zucchini; diced carrot; or diced celery.

In medium bowl, combine ground beef, Italian seasoning and ¼ teaspoon garlic powder. Shape into 1-inch meatballs.

In 6-quart Dutch oven or heavy saucepan, heat 1 tablespoon oil over medium-high heat and brown meatballs. Remove meatballs. Heat remaining 1 tablespoon oil in same Dutch oven and cook vegetables, stirring frequently, 5 minutes or until crisp-tender. Stir in soup mix blended with water, remaining ¼ teaspoon garlic powder, tomatoes and sugar. Bring to a boil over high heat, breaking up tomatoes with wooden spoon. Reduce heat to low and simmer covered 25 minutes. Return meatballs to skillet. Continue simmering covered 5 minutes or until meatballs are heated through. Serve with grated Parmesan cheese and garlic bread, if desired.

makes 6 servings

chicken parmesan hero sandwiches

4 boneless, skinless chicken breast halves (about 1¼ pounds)

1 egg, slightly beaten

¾ cup Italian seasoned dry bread crumbs

1 jar (26 to 28 ounces) RAGÚ® Old World Style® Pasta Sauce

1 cup shredded mozzarella cheese (about 4 ounces)

4 long Italian rolls, halved lengthwise

1. Preheat oven to 400°F. Dip chicken in egg, then bread crumbs, coating well.

2. In 13×9-inch glass baking dish, arrange chicken. Bake uncovered 20 minutes.

3. Pour Ragú Pasta Sauce over chicken, then top with cheese. Bake an additional 10 minutes or until chicken is no longer pink. To serve, arrange chicken and sauce on rolls.

makes 4 servings

prep time: 10 minutes
cook time: 30 minutes

easy kids' taco-mac

1 pound ground turkey

1 package (1.0 ounce) LAWRY'S® Taco Spices & Seasonings

1 can (14½ ounces) whole peeled tomatoes, undrained and cut up

1 cup water

8 ounces dry macaroni or small spiral pasta

½ cup sliced celery

1 package (8½ ounces) corn muffin mix

1 egg

⅓ cup milk

In medium skillet, brown ground turkey until crumbly. Add Taco Spices & Seasonings, tomatoes, water, pasta and celery; mix well. Bring to a boil over medium-high heat; reduce heat to low and simmer covered 20 minutes. In medium bowl, combine corn muffin mix, egg and milk; stir with fork just to mix. Place turkey mixture in 2½-quart casserole dish. Spoon dollops of corn muffin mix on top. Bake in 400°F oven 15 to 20 minutes or until golden.

makes 6 to 8 servings

serving suggestion: Sprinkle with grated cheese.

chicken parmesan hero sandwich

by-the-sea casserole

- 1 bag (16 ounces) BIRDS EYE® frozen Mixed Vegetables
- 2 cans (6 ounces each) tuna in water, drained
- 1 cup uncooked instant rice
- 1 can (10¾ ounces) cream of celery soup
- 1 cup 1% milk
- 1 cup cheese-flavored fish-shaped crackers

• In medium bowl, combine vegetables and tuna.

• Stir in rice, soup and milk.

• Place tuna mixture in 1½-quart microwave-safe casserole dish; cover and microwave on HIGH 6 minutes. Stir; microwave, covered, 6 to 8 minutes more or until rice is tender.

• Stir casserole and sprinkle with crackers.   *makes 6 servings*

birds eye idea: Need to cut salt out of your diet? Add spices and herbs instead.

prep time: 10 minutes
cook time: 15 minutes

souper quick "lasagna"

- 1½ pounds ground beef
- 1 envelope LIPTON® RECIPE SECRETS® Onion or Onion-Mushroom Soup Mix
- 3 cans (8 ounces each) tomato sauce
- 1 cup water
- ½ teaspoon dried oregano leaves (optional)
- 1 package (8 ounces) broad egg noodles, cooked and drained
- 1 package (16 ounces) mozzarella cheese, shredded

Preheat oven to 375°F.

In 12-inch skillet, brown ground beef over medium-high heat; drain. Stir in onion soup mix, tomato sauce, water and oregano. Simmer covered, stirring occasionally, 15 minutes.

In 2-quart oblong baking dish spoon enough sauce to cover bottom. Alternately layer noodles, ground beef mixture and cheese, ending with cheese. Bake 30 minutes or until bubbling.   *makes about 6 servings*

microwave directions: In 2-quart casserole, microwave ground beef, uncovered, at HIGH (Full Power) 7 minutes, stirring once; drain. Stir in onion soup mix, tomato sauce, water and oregano. Microwave at MEDIUM (50% Power) 5 minutes, stirring once. In 2-quart oblong baking dish, spoon enough sauce to cover bottom. Alternately layer as above. Microwave covered at MEDIUM, turning dish occasionally, 10 minutes or until bubbling. Let stand covered 5 minutes.

200

hot diggity dots & twisters

⅔ cup milk

2 tablespoons margarine or butter

1 (4.8-ounce) package PASTA RONI® Four Cheese Flavor with Corkscrew Pasta

1½ cups frozen peas

4 hot dogs, cut into ½-inch pieces

2 teaspoons mustard

1. In large saucepan, bring 1¼ cups water, milk and margarine just to a boil.

2. Stir in pasta, peas and Special Seasonings; return to a boil. Reduce heat to medium. Gently boil uncovered, 7 to 8 minutes or until pasta is tender, stirring occasionally.

3. Stir in hot dogs and mustard. Let stand 3 to 5 minutes before serving. *makes 4 servings*

prep time: 5 minutes
cook time: 15 minutes

chicken rice casserole

4 tablespoons butter, divided

4 boneless skinless chicken breasts

1½ cups uncooked converted rice

6 ounces HILLSHIRE FARM® Lit'l Smokies

1 can (about 14 ounces) cream of chicken soup

1 can (about 14 ounces) cream of celery soup

1 cup sliced mushrooms

½ cup dry sherry

Bread crumbs

Cheddar cheese

Slivered almonds

Preheat oven to 275°F.

Melt 2 tablespoons butter in large skillet over medium-high heat. Add chicken; sauté until cooked through, about 7 minutes on each side. Remove chicken and cut into bite-size pieces.

Place rice on bottom of medium casserole; add chicken, Lit'l Smokies, soups, ¾ cup water, mushrooms, sherry and remaining 2 tablespoons butter. Bake, covered, 2½ hours. Top casserole with bread crumbs, cheese and almonds. Broil until golden brown and cheese is melted.

makes 6 to 8 servings

tip: Be sure to avoid overcooking—it's the major pitfall of casseroles destined for the freezer. A simple way is to undercook any pasta or rice; it will cook through when the casserole is reheated.

203

chuckwagon bbq rice round-up

1 pound lean ground beef

1 (6.8-ounce) package RICE-A-RONI® Beef Flavor

2 tablespoons margarine or butter

2 cups frozen corn

½ cup prepared barbecue sauce

½ cup (2 ounces) shredded Cheddar cheese

1. In large skillet over medium-high heat, brown ground beef until well cooked. Remove from skillet; drain. Set aside.

2. In same skillet over medium heat, sauté rice-vermicelli mix with margarine until vermicelli is golden brown.

3. Slowly stir in 2½ cups water, corn and Special Seasonings; bring to a boil. Reduce heat to low. Cover; simmer 15 to 20 minutes or until rice is tender.

4. Stir in barbecue sauce and ground beef. Sprinkle with cheese. Cover; let stand 3 to 5 minutes or until cheese is melted.

makes 4 servings

tip: Salsa can be substituted for barbecue sauce.

prep time: 5 minutes
cook time: 25 minutes

funny face pizzas

1 package (10 ounces) refrigerated pizza dough

1 cup pizza sauce

1 cup (4 ounces) shredded mozzarella cheese

Assorted toppings: pepperoni, black olive slices, green or red bell pepper slices, mushroom slices

⅓ cup shredded Cheddar cheese

Heat oven to 425°F. Spray baking sheet with nonstick cooking spray; set aside.

Remove dough from package. *Do not unroll dough.* Slice dough into 4 equal pieces. Knead each piece of dough until ball forms. Pat or roll each ball into 4-inch disk. Place disks on prepared baking sheet.

Spread ¼ cup sauce on each disk. Sprinkle with mozzarella cheese. Decorate with toppings to create faces. Sprinkle with Cheddar cheese to resemble hair.

Bake 10 minutes or until cheese is just melted and bottoms of pizzas are light brown.

makes 4 servings

COOKIES

honey bees

¾ **cup shortening**

½ **cup sugar**

¼ **cup honey**

 1 **egg**

½ **teaspoon vanilla**

 2 **cups all-purpose flour**

⅓ **cup cornmeal**

 1 **teaspoon baking powder**

½ **teaspoon salt**

 Yellow and black icings or gels and gummy fruit

1. Beat shortening, sugar and honey in large bowl at medium speed of electric mixer until fluffy. Add egg and vanilla; mix until well blended.

2. Combine flour, cornmeal, baking powder and salt in medium bowl. Add to shortening mixture; mix at low speed until well blended.

3. Cover; refrigerate several hours or overnight, if desired.

4. Preheat oven to 375°F. Divide dough into 24 equal sections.

5. Shape each section into oval-shaped ball. Place 2 inches apart on ungreased cookie sheets.

6. Bake 10 to 12 minutes or until lightly browned. Cool 2 minutes on cookie sheets. Remove to wire racks; cool completely.

7. Decorate with icings, gels and gummy fruit to create honey bees.

makes 2 dozen cookies

super chocolate cookies

2 cups all-purpose flour

⅓ cup unsweetened cocoa powder

1 teaspoon baking soda

½ teaspoon salt

½ cup butter, softened

½ cup shortening

1⅓ cups packed brown sugar

2 eggs

2 teaspoons vanilla

1 cup candy-coated chocolate pieces

1 cup raisins

¾ cup salted peanuts, coarsely chopped

1. Preheat oven to 350°F. Combine flour, cocoa, baking soda and salt in medium bowl; set aside.

2. Beat butter, shortening and brown sugar in large bowl of electric mixer at medium speed until light and fluffy. Beat in eggs and vanilla until well blended. Gradually add flour mixture, beating at low speed until blended. Stir in candy pieces, raisins and peanuts.

3. Drop dough by ¼ cupfuls onto ungreased cookie sheets, spacing 3 inches apart. Flatten slightly with fingertips. Bake cookies 13 to 15 minutes or until almost set. Cool 2 minutes on cookie sheets. Transfer to wire racks. Cool completely.

makes 18 to 20 (4-inch) cookies

banana peanut jumbles

2 ripe, medium DOLE® Bananas

½ cup packed brown sugar

½ cup peanut butter

½ cup roasted peanuts

1⅓ cups buttermilk baking mix

1 tablespoon water

• **Mash** bananas; measure 1 cup.

• **Combine** bananas, brown sugar, peanut butter and peanuts. Add baking mix and water. Stir until well blended.

• **Drop** batter by heaping tablespoonfuls onto cookie sheets coated with cooking spray.

• **Bake** at 350°F 20 to 25 minutes or until golden. Cool on rack.

makes 18 cookies

prep time: 15 minutes
bake time: 25 minutes

208

golden peanut butter bars

2 cups all-purpose flour

¾ cup firmly packed
 light brown sugar

1 egg, beaten

½ cup (1 stick) cold
 butter or margarine

1 cup finely chopped
 peanuts

1 (14-ounce) can
 EAGLE® BRAND
 Sweetened
 Condensed Milk
 (NOT evaporated
 milk)

½ cup peanut butter

1 teaspoon vanilla
 extract

1. Preheat oven to 350°F. Combine flour, sugar and egg in large bowl; cut in cold butter until crumbly. Stir in peanuts. Reserve 2 cups crumb mixture. Press remaining mixture on bottom of 13×9-inch baking pan.

2. Bake 15 minutes or until lightly browned.

3. Meanwhile, beat Eagle Brand, peanut butter and vanilla in another large bowl. Spread over prepared crust; top with reserved crumb mixture.

4. Bake an additional 25 minutes or until lightly browned. Cool. Cut into bars. Store covered at room temperature.   *makes 24 to 36 bars*

prep time: 20 minutes
bake time: 40 minutes

3-minute no-bake cookies

2 cups granulated sugar

½ cup (1 stick)
 margarine or butter

½ cup 2% milk

⅓ cup unsweetened
 cocoa powder

3 cups QUAKER® Oats
 (quick or old
 fashioned,
 uncooked)

In large saucepan, combine sugar, margarine, milk and cocoa. Bring to boil over medium heat, stirring frequently. Continue boiling 3 minutes. Remove from heat. Stir in oats; mix well. Quickly drop by tablespoonfuls onto waxed paper or greased cookie sheet. Let stand until set. Store tightly covered at room temperature.   *makes about 3 dozen cookies*

210

lollipop sugar cookies

1¼ cups granulated sugar

1 cup Butter Flavor CRISCO® all-vegetable shortening or 1 Butter Flavor CRISCO® Stick

2 eggs

¼ cup light corn syrup or regular pancake syrup

1 tablespoon vanilla

3 cups all-purpose flour

¾ teaspoon baking powder

½ teaspoon baking soda

½ teaspoon salt

36 flat ice cream sticks

Any of the following: miniature baking chips, raisins, red hots, nonpareils, colored sugar or nuts

1. Combine sugar and shortening in large bowl. Beat at medium speed of electric mixer until well blended. Add eggs, syrup and vanilla; beat until well blended and fluffy.

2. Combine flour, baking powder, baking soda and salt. Add gradually to creamed mixture at low speed until well blended. Wrap dough in plastic wrap. Refrigerate at least 1 hour.

3. Heat oven to 375°F. Place foil on countertop for cooling cookies.

4. Shape dough into 1½-inch balls. Push ice cream stick into center of each ball. Place balls 3 inches apart on ungreased baking sheet. Flatten balls to ½-inch thickness with bottom of greased and floured glass. Decorate as desired; press decorations gently into dough.*

5. Bake at 375°F for 8 to 10 minutes. *Do not overbake.* Cool on baking sheet 2 minutes. Remove cookies to foil to cool completely.

makes about 3 dozen cookies

*Cookies can also be painted before baking. Mix 1 egg yolk and ¼ teaspoon water. Divide into 3 small cups. Add 2 to 3 drops food color to each. Stir. Use clean water color brushes to paint designs on cookies.

chocolate teddy bears

⅔ cup butter or
  margarine, softened

1 cup sugar

2 teaspoons vanilla
  extract

2 eggs

2½ cups all-purpose flour

½ cup HERSHEY'S
  Cocoa

½ teaspoon baking soda

¼ teaspoon salt

1. Beat butter, sugar and vanilla in large bowl until fluffy. Add eggs; beat well. Stir together flour, cocoa, baking soda and salt; gradually add to butter mixture, blending thoroughly. Refrigerate until dough is firm enough to handle.

2. Heat oven to 350°F.

3. To shape teddy bears: For each cookie, form a portion of the dough into 1 large ball for body (1 to 1½ inches), 1 medium-size ball for head (¾ to 1 inch), 4 small balls for arms and legs (½ inch), 2 smaller balls for ears, 1 tiny ball for nose and 4 tiny balls for paws (optional). On ungreased cookie sheet flatten large ball slightly for body. Attach medium-size ball for head by overlapping slightly onto body. Place balls for arms, legs and ears, and a tiny ball on head for nose. Arrange other tiny balls atop ends of legs and arms for paws, if desired. With wooden pick, draw eyes and mouth; pierce small hole at top of cookie for use as hanging ornament, if desired.

4. Bake 6 to 8 minutes or until set. Cool 1 minute; remove from cookie sheet to wire rack. Cool completely. Store in covered container. If cookies will be used as ornaments, allow to dry on wire rack at least 6 hours before hanging. Pull ribbon through hole for hanging, if desired.

makes about 14 cookies

p.b. swirls

½ cup shortening

1 cup sugar

½ cup crunchy peanut
  butter

1 egg

2 teaspoons milk

1¼ cups sifted flour

½ teaspoon salt

½ teaspoon baking soda

1 (6-ounce) package
  chocolate chips

Preheat oven to 375°F. Cream shortening and sugar. Beat in peanut butter, egg and milk. In separate bowl, mix flour, salt and baking soda. Mix dry ingredients into peanut butter mixture. Place dough on lightly greased waxed paper. Using your hands, shape dough into a rectangle. Melt chocolate chips and spread over dough. Starting at long edge, roll up dough like a jelly roll. Chill ½ hour. Slice into ¼-inch slices. Place on ungreased cookie sheet. Bake at 375°F for 8 to 10 minutes.

makes 2 dozen cookies

Favorite recipe from **Peanut Advisory Board**

butterfly cookies

2¼ cups all-purpose flour

¼ teaspoon salt

1 cup sugar

¾ cup (1½ sticks) butter, softened

1 egg

1 teaspoon vanilla

1 teaspoon almond extract

White frosting, assorted food colorings, colored sugars, assorted small decors, gummy fruit and hard candies for decoration

1. Combine flour and salt in medium bowl; set aside.

2. Beat sugar and butter in large bowl at medium speed of electric mixer until fluffy. Beat in egg, vanilla and almond extract. Gradually add flour mixture. Beat at low speed until well blended. Divide dough in half. Cover; refrigerate 30 minutes or until firm.

3. Preheat oven to 350°F. Grease cookie sheets. Roll half of dough on lightly floured surface to ¼-inch thickness. Cut out cookies using butterfly cookie cutters. Repeat with remaining dough.

4. Bake 12 to 15 minutes or until edges are lightly browned. Remove to wire racks; cool completely.

5. Tint portions of white frosting with assorted food colorings. Spread desired colors of frosting over cookies. Decorate as desired.

makes about 20 to 22 cookies

When making cut-out cookies, lightly coat your cookie cutters with nonstick cooking spray before using them so the dough won't stick to the cutters. Or, dip them in flour before cutting out the dough.

giant peanut butter cup cookies

½ cup (1 stick) butter or margarine, softened

¾ cup sugar

⅓ cup REESE'S® Creamy or Crunchy Peanut Butter

1 egg

½ teaspoon vanilla extract

1¼ cups all-purpose flour

½ teaspoon baking soda

¼ teaspoon salt

16 REESE'S® Peanut Butter Cup Miniatures, cut into fourths

1. Heat oven to 350°F.

2. Beat butter, sugar and peanut butter in medium bowl until creamy. Add egg and vanilla; beat well. Stir together flour, baking soda and salt. Add to butter mixture; blend well. Drop dough by level ¼ cup measurements onto ungreased cookie sheets, three cookies per sheet. (Cookies will spread while baking.) Push about seven pieces of peanut butter cup into each cookie, flattening cookie slightly.

3. Bake 15 to 17 minutes or until light golden brown around the edges. Centers will be pale and slightly soft. Cool 1 minute on cookie sheet. Remove to wire rack; cool completely. *makes 9 cookies*

sugar cookie pizza

1 package DUNCAN HINES® Golden Sugar Cookie Mix

½ cup semisweet mini chocolate coated candy pieces

1 container DUNCAN HINES® Vanilla or Chocolate Frosting (optional)

Preheat oven to 350°F.

Prepare cookie mix as directed on package. Spread onto lightly greased 12-inch pizza pan. Sprinkle candy pieces evenly over cookie dough; press down gently. Bake 15 to 20 minutes or until golden brown. Cool 3 to 4 minutes in pan. Remove from pan; cool completely. Decorate with frosting, if desired. *makes 12 servings*

chocolate nut bars

1¾ cups graham cracker crumbs

½ cup butter or margarine, melted

1 (14-ounce) can EAGLE® BRAND Sweetened Condensed Milk (NOT evaporated milk)

2 cups (12 ounces) semi-sweet chocolate chips, divided

1 teaspoon vanilla extract

1 cup chopped nuts

1. Preheat oven to 375°F. Combine crumbs and butter; press firmly on bottom of 13×9-inch baking pan. Bake 8 minutes. Reduce oven temperature to 350°F.

2. In small saucepan, melt Eagle Brand with 1 cup chocolate chips and vanilla. Spread chocolate mixture over prepared crust. Top with remaining 1 cup chocolate chips, then nuts; press down firmly.

3. Bake 25 to 30 minutes. Cool. Chill if desired. Cut into bars. Store loosely covered at room temperature. *makes 24 to 36 bars*

prep time: 10 minutes
bake time: 33 to 38 minutes

snowball cookies

1 cup margarine or butter, softened

1 cup sugar

1 teaspoon vanilla extract

2 cups all-purpose flour

1½ cups PLANTERS® Pecans, finely ground

¼ teaspoon salt

½ cup powdered sugar

1. Beat margarine or butter, sugar and vanilla in large bowl with mixer at medium speed until creamy. Blend in flour, pecans and salt. Refrigerate 1 hour.

2. Shape dough into 1-inch balls. Place on ungreased baking sheets, 2 inches apart. Bake in preheated 350°F oven for 10 to 12 minutes. Remove from sheets; cool on wire racks. Dust with powdered sugar. Store in airtight container. *makes 6 dozen cookies*

preparation time: 15 minutes
chill time: 1 hour
cook time: 10 minutes
total time: 1 hour and 25 minutes

218

banana split sundae cookies

1 cup (2 sticks)
   margarine or butter,
   softened

1 cup firmly packed
   brown sugar

1½ cups mashed ripe
   bananas (about
   4 medium)

2 eggs

2 teaspoons vanilla

2½ cups QUAKER® Oats
   (quick or old
   fashioned,
   uncooked)

2 cups all-purpose flour

1 teaspoon baking soda

¼ teaspoon salt
   (optional)

1 cup (6 ounces)
   semisweet
   chocolate pieces

Ice cream or frozen
   yogurt

Ice cream topping,
   any flavor

Heat oven to 350°F. Beat together margarine and sugar until creamy. Add bananas, eggs and vanilla; beat well. Add combined oats, flour, baking soda and salt; mix well. Stir in chocolate pieces; mix well. Drop by ¼ cupfuls onto ungreased cookie sheet about 3 inches apart. Spread dough to 3½-inch diameter. Bake 14 to 16 minutes or until edges are light golden brown. Cool 1 minute on cookie sheet; remove to wire rack. Cool completely. To serve, top each cookie with a scoop of ice cream and ice cream topping.   *makes about 2 dozen cookies*

To ripen bananas, store them uncovered at room temperature. You can speed up the ripening process by placing them in a brown paper bag with a ripe apple. If the bananas ripen before you're ready to use them, just place them in a resealable plastic food storage bag in the refrigerator—the peel will turn a dark brown but the flesh inside will not change at all and is perfectly good to eat.

heavenly oat bars

MAZOLA NO STICK®
Cooking Spray

½ **cup (1 stick)**
margarine or butter,
softened

½ **cup firmly packed**
brown sugar

½ **cup KARO® Light or**
Dark Corn Syrup

1 teaspoon vanilla

3 cups uncooked quick
or old-fashioned
oats

1 cup (6 ounces) semi-
sweet chocolate
chips

½ **cup SKIPPY® Creamy**
Peanut Butter

1. Preheat oven to 350°F. Spray 9-inch square baking pan with cooking spray.

2. In large bowl with mixer at medium speed, beat margarine, brown sugar, corn syrup and vanilla until blended and smooth. Stir in oats. Spread in prepared pan.

3. Bake 25 minutes or until center is just firm. Cool slightly on wire rack.

4. In small heavy saucepan over low heat, stir chocolate chips until melted and smooth. Remove from heat; stir in peanut butter until smooth. Spread over warm bars. Cool completely in pan on wire rack before cutting.   *makes about 2 dozen bars*

tip: To melt chocolate chips in microwave, place in dry microwavable bowl or glass measuring cup. Microwave on HIGH (100% power) 1 minute; stir. Microwave on HIGH 1 minute longer. Stir until chocolate is smooth.

prep time: 15 minutes
bake time: 25 minutes, plus cooling

dino-mite dinosaurs

1 cup (2 sticks) butter, softened

1¼ cups granulated sugar

1 large egg

2 squares (1 ounce each) semi-sweet chocolate, melted

½ teaspoon vanilla extract

2⅓ cups all-purpose flour

1 teaspoon baking powder

¼ teaspoon salt

1 cup white frosting

Assorted food colorings

1 cup "M&M's"® Chocolate Mini Baking Bits

In large bowl cream butter and sugar until light and fluffy; beat in egg, chocolate and vanilla. In medium bowl combine flour, baking powder and salt; add to creamed mixture. Wrap and refrigerate dough 2 to 3 hours. Preheat oven to 350°F. Working with half the dough at a time on lightly floured surface, roll to ¼-inch thickness. Cut into dinosaur shapes using 4-inch cookie cutters. Place about 2 inches apart on ungreased cookie sheets. Bake 10 to 12 minutes. Cool 2 minutes on cookie sheets; cool completely on wire racks. Tint frosting desired colors. Frost cookies and decorate with "M&M's"® Chocolate Mini Baking Bits. Store in tightly covered container.

makes 2 dozen cookies

devil's food fudge cookies

1 package DUNCAN HINES® Moist Deluxe® Devil's Food Cake Mix

2 eggs

½ cup vegetable oil

1 cup semisweet chocolate chips

½ cup chopped walnuts

1. Preheat oven to 350°F. Grease baking sheets.

2. Combine cake mix, eggs and oil in large bowl. Stir until thoroughly blended. Stir in chocolate chips and walnuts. (Mixture will be stiff.) Shape dough into 36 (1¼-inch) balls. Place 2 inches apart on prepared baking sheets.

3. Bake at 350°F for 10 to 11 minutes. (Cookies will look moist.) *Do not overbake.* Cool 2 minutes on baking sheets. Remove to cooling racks. Cool completely. Store in airtight container.

makes 3 dozen cookies

caramel nut chocolate cookies

1½ cups firmly packed light brown sugar

⅔ CRISCO® Stick or ⅔ cup CRISCO® all-vegetable shortening

1 tablespoon water

1 teaspoon vanilla

2 eggs

1¾ cups all-purpose flour

⅓ cup unsweetened cocoa powder

½ teaspoon salt

¼ teaspoon baking soda

2 cups (12 ounces) miniature semisweet chocolate chips

1 cup chopped pecans

20 to 25 caramels, unwrapped and halved

1. Heat oven to 375°F. Place sheets of foil on countertop for cooling cookies.

2. Place brown sugar, shortening, water and vanilla in large bowl. Beat at medium speed of electric mixer until well blended. Add eggs; beat well.

3. Combine flour, cocoa, salt and baking soda. Add to shortening mixture; beat at low speed just until blended. Stir in chocolate chips.

4. Shape dough into 1¼-inch balls. Dip tops in chopped pecans. Place 2 inches apart on ungreased baking sheet. Press caramel half in center of each ball.

5. Bake one baking sheet at a time at 375°F for 7 to 9 minutes or until cookies are set. *Do not overbake.* Cool 2 minutes on baking sheet. Remove cookies to foil to cool completely.

makes about 4 dozen cookies

224

oatmeal surprise cookies

1 cup all-purpose flour

½ teaspoon baking soda

½ teaspoon salt

½ teaspoon ground cinnamon

½ cup butter, softened

⅓ cup granulated sugar

⅓ cup firmly packed brown sugar

1 egg, at room temperature

½ cup quick-cooking oats

⅓ cup KNOTT'S® Berry Farm Preserves, any flavor

1. Preheat oven to 350°F.

2. In small bowl, combine flour, baking soda, salt and cinnamon; set aside.

3. In large bowl, cream together butter and sugars; beat in egg.

4. Gradually add flour mixture until blended. Stir in oats. Refrigerate 15 minutes.

5. Roll heaping *teaspoon* dough into a ball, then flatten to ¼-inch thickness.

6. Place dough on cookie sheet; top with *1 teaspoon* Knott's Preserves.

7. Roll another *teaspoon* of dough into a ball, flatten to ¼-inch thickness and place over preserves.

8. Press around outer edges to seal. Repeat with remaining dough and preserves.

9. Bake 10 to 12 minutes or until edges start to brown.

makes 18 cookies

crispy cut-outs

1 (10-ounce) package JET-PUFFED® Marshmallows or 1 (10.5-ounce) package JET-PUFFED® Miniature Marshmallows

6 cups crisp rice cereal

Decorator icing, candies and sprinkles, for decorating

1. Place marshmallows in lightly greased large microwavable bowl. Microwave at HIGH (100% power) for 1½ minutes or until melted and smooth, stirring after 45 seconds.

2. Immediately stir in cereal to coat completely; press into greased 15×10×1-inch pan. Let mixture cool 10 minutes. Refrigerate for 1 hour.

3. Cut into assorted holiday shapes with greased holiday-shaped cookie cutters. If desired, use toothpick to make hole at top of cut-out; thread ribbon through hole and tie into bow for hanging. Decorate cut-outs with icings, assorted candies and sprinkles.

makes about 1½ dozen cut-outs

chocolate cherry bars

1 cup (2 sticks) butter or margarine

¾ cup HERSHEY'S Cocoa or HERSHEY'S Dutch Processed Cocoa

2 cups sugar

4 eggs

1½ cups plus ⅓ cup all-purpose flour, divided

⅓ cup chopped almonds

1 can (14 ounces) sweetened condensed milk (not evaporated milk)

½ teaspoon almond extract

1 cup HERSHEY'S MINI KISSES™ Semi-Sweet or Milk Chocolate Baking Pieces

1 cup chopped maraschino cherries, drained

1. Heat oven to 350°F. Generously grease 13×9×2-inch baking pan.

2. Melt butter in large saucepan over low heat; stir in cocoa until smooth. Remove from heat. Add sugar, 3 eggs, 1½ cups flour and almonds; mix well. Pour into prepared pan. Bake 20 minutes.

3. Meanwhile, whisk together remaining 1 egg, remaining ⅓ cup flour, sweetened condensed milk and almond extract. Pour over baked layer; sprinkle Mini Kisses™ and cherries over top. Return to oven.

4. Bake additional 20 to 25 minutes or until set and edges are golden brown. Cool completely in pan on wire rack. Refrigerate until cold, 6 hours or overnight. Cut into bars. Cover; refrigerate leftover bars.

makes about 48 bars

Dutch-processed cocoa has been alkalized, which neutralizes the cocoa's natural acidity. It has a darker color and mellower flavor than regular cocoa powder. Cocoa should be sealed airtight and stored in a cool, dark place; it will keep for up to 2 years.

magic cookie bars

½ cup (1 stick) butter or margarine

1½ cups graham cracker crumbs

1 (14-ounce) can EAGLE® BRAND Sweetened Condensed Milk (NOT evaporated milk)

2 cups (12 ounces) semi-sweet chocolate chips

1⅓ cups flaked coconut

1 cup chopped nuts

1. Preheat oven to 350°F (325°F for glass dish). In 13×9-inch baking pan, melt butter in oven.

2. Sprinkle crumbs over butter; pour Eagle Brand evenly over crumbs. Layer evenly with remaining ingredients; press down firmly.

3. Bake 25 minutes or until lightly browned. Cool. Chill if desired. Cut into bars. Store loosely covered at room temperature.

makes 24 to 36 bars

bake time: 25 minutes

7-layer magic cookie bars: Substitute 1 cup (6 ounces) butterscotch-flavored chips for 1 cup semi-sweet chocolate chips and proceed as directed above.

magic peanut cookie bars: Substitute 2 cups (about ¾ pound) chocolate-covered peanuts for semi-sweet chocolate chips and chopped nuts.

magic rainbow cookie bars: Substitute 2 cups plain candy-coated chocolate pieces for semi-sweet chocolate chips.

cinnamon stars

2 tablespoons sugar

¾ teaspoon ground cinnamon

¾ cup butter or margarine, softened

2 egg yolks

1 teaspoon vanilla extract

1 package DUNCAN HINES® Moist Deluxe® French Vanilla Cake Mix

1. Preheat oven to 375°F. Combine sugar and cinnamon in small bowl. Set aside.

2. Combine butter, egg yolks and vanilla extract in large bowl. Blend in cake mix gradually. Roll to ⅛-inch thickness on lightly floured surface. Cut with 2½-inch star cookie cutter. Place 2 inches apart on ungreased baking sheet.

3. Sprinkle cookies with cinnamon-sugar mixture. Bake at 375°F for 6 to 8 minutes or until edges are light golden brown. Cool 1 minute on baking sheet. Remove to cooling rack. Cool completely. Store in airtight container. *makes 3 to 3½ dozen cookies*

tip: You can use your favorite cookie cutter in place of the star cookie cutter.

teddy granola snack bars

9 HONEY MAID® Honey Graham squares

1½ cups TEDDY GRAHAM® Graham Snacks, any flavor, divided

¾ cup quick-cooking oats

½ cup PLANTERS® Dry Roasted Peanuts, chopped

½ cup diced dried fruit mix

½ cup packed light brown sugar

⅓ cup margarine or butter, melted

2 eggs

1. Arrange 9 graham squares in greased 8×8×2-inch baking pan. Layer 1 cup graham snacks, oats, peanuts and fruit mix over grahams; top with remaining graham snacks.

2. Mix brown sugar, margarine or butter and eggs in small bowl until smooth; pour evenly over mixture in pan.

3. Bake at 350°F for 20 to 25 minutes or until golden. Cool completely in pan on wire rack. Cut into bars. *makes 16 bars*

colorific chocolate chip cookies

1 cup (2 sticks) butter or margarine, softened

⅔ cup granulated sugar

½ cup firmly packed light brown sugar

1 large egg

1 teaspoon vanilla extract

2 cups all-purpose flour

¾ teaspoon baking soda

¾ teaspoon salt

1¾ cups "M&M's"® Semi-Sweet Chocolate Mini Baking Bits

¾ cup chopped nuts, optional

Preheat oven to 375°F. In large bowl cream butter and sugars until light and fluffy; beat in egg and vanilla. In medium bowl combine flour, baking soda and salt; blend into creamed mixture. Stir in "M&M's"® Semi-Sweet Chocolate Mini Baking Bits and nuts, if using. Drop by heaping tablespoonfuls about 2 inches apart onto ungreased cookie sheets. Bake 9 to 12 minutes or until lightly browned. Cool 1 minute on cookie sheets; cool completely on wire racks. Store in tightly covered container.   *makes about 3 dozen cookies*

hint: For chewy cookies bake 9 to 10 minutes; for crispy cookies bake 11 to 12 minutes.

pan cookie variation: Prepare dough as directed; spread into lightly greased 15×10×1-inch jelly-roll pan. Bake at 375°F for 18 to 22 minutes. Cool completely before cutting into 35 (2-inch) squares. For a more festive look, reserve ½ cup baking bits to sprinkle on top of dough before baking.

triple chipper monsters

2½ cups all-purpose flour

1 teaspoon baking soda

¾ teaspoon salt

1 cup butter, softened

1 cup packed light brown sugar

½ cup granulated sugar

2 eggs

2 teaspoons vanilla

2 cups semisweet chocolate chips

½ cup white chocolate chips

½ cup butterscotch or peanut butter chips

1. Preheat oven to 350°F.

2. Combine flour, baking soda and salt in medium bowl; set aside.

3. Beat butter, brown sugar and granulated sugar in large bowl of electric mixer at medium speed until light and fluffy. Beat in eggs and vanilla until blended. Gradually beat in flour mixture on low speed until well blended. Stir in chips.

4. Drop dough by scant ¼ cupfuls onto ungreased cookie sheets, spacing 3 inches apart. Lightly flatten dough with fingertips. Bake 12 to 14 minutes or until edges are set and golden brown. Cool cookies 1 to 2 minutes on cookie sheets; transfer to wire racks. Cool completely.   *makes about 22 (4-inch) cookies*

232

choco-scutterbotch

⅔ **Butter Flavor CRISCO®**
  Stick or ⅔ cup
  Butter Flavor
  CRISCO®
  all-vegetable
  shortening

½ **cup firmly packed**
  brown sugar

2 **eggs**

1 **package (18¼ ounces)**
  deluxe yellow cake
  mix

1 **cup toasted rice**
  cereal

½ **cup butterscotch**
  chips

½ **cup milk chocolate**
  chunks

½ **cup semisweet**
  chocolate chips

½ **cup coarsely chopped**
  walnuts or pecans

1. Heat oven to 375°F. Place sheets of foil on countertop for cooling cookies.

2. Combine ⅔ cup shortening and brown sugar in large bowl. Beat at medium speed with electric mixer until well blended. Beat in eggs.

3. Add cake mix gradually at low speed. Mix until well blended. Stir in cereal, butterscotch chips, chocolate chunks, chocolate chips and nuts. Stir until well blended.

4. Shape dough into 1¼-inch balls. Place 2 inches apart on ungreased baking sheet. Flatten slightly. Shape sides to form circle, if necessary.

5. Bake for 7 to 9 minutes or until lightly browned around edges. *Do not overbake.* Cool 2 minutes on baking sheet. Remove cookies to foil to cool completely.   *makes 3 dozen cookies*

If you know you'll always have hungry kids around, keep an extra batch of cookies in the freezer for "emergencies". Store cookies in resealable plastic freezer bags, or in airtight plastic containers with sheets of waxed paper between layers. Cookies can be frozen for 4 to 6 months—but they'll probably be eaten long before then!

cocoa snickerdoodles

1 cup butter, softened
¾ cup packed brown sugar
¾ cup plus 2 tablespoons granulated sugar, divided
2 eggs
2 cups uncooked old-fashioned oats
1½ cups all-purpose flour
¼ cup plus 2 tablespoons unsweetened cocoa powder, divided
1 teaspoon baking soda
2 tablespoons ground cinnamon

Preheat oven to 375°F. Lightly grease cookie sheets or line with parchment paper.

Beat butter, brown sugar and ¾ cup granulated sugar in large bowl until light and fluffy. Add eggs; mix well. Combine oats, flour, ¼ cup cocoa and baking soda in medium bowl. Stir into butter mixture until blended.

Mix remaining 2 tablespoons granulated sugar, remaining 2 tablespoons cocoa and cinnamon in small bowl. Drop dough by rounded teaspoonfuls into cinnamon mixture; toss to coat. Place 2 inches apart on prepared cookie sheets.

Bake 8 to 10 minutes or until firm in center. *Do not overbake.* Remove to wire racks to cool. *makes about 4½ dozen cookies*

brownie cookie bites

1½ cups (9 ounces) NESTLÉ® TOLL HOUSE® Semi-Sweet Chocolate Morsels, *divided*
1 tablespoon butter
¼ cup all-purpose flour
¼ teaspoon baking powder
1 large egg
⅓ cup granulated sugar
½ teaspoon vanilla extract

Melt ½ cup morsels and butter over hot (not boiling) water, stirring until smooth. Combine flour and baking powder in small bowl.

Beat egg and sugar in large mixer bowl at high speed about 3 minutes or until mixture has thickened. Stir in vanilla extract and melted chocolate mixture. Gradually blend in flour mixture. Stir in remaining 1 cup morsels. Drop by level tablespoon onto greased baking sheets.

Bake in preheated 350°F. oven for 8 to 10 minutes or until cookies are puffed and tops are cracked and moist (cookies will look slightly underbaked). Cool on baking sheets for 5 minutes. Remove to wire racks to cool completely. *makes about 1½ dozen cookies*

domino cookies

1 package (20 ounces)
  refrigerated sugar
  cookie dough
All-purpose flour
  (optional)
½ cup semisweet
  chocolate chips

1. Preheat oven to 350°F. Grease cookie sheets.

2. Remove dough from wrapper according to package directions. Cut dough into 4 equal sections. Reserve 1 section; refrigerate remaining 3 sections.

3. Roll reserved dough to ⅛-inch thickness. Sprinkle with flour to minimize sticking, if necessary. Cut out 9 (2½×1¾-inch) rectangles using sharp knife. Place 2 inches apart on prepared cookie sheets.

4. Score each cookie across middle with sharp knife. Gently press chocolate chips, point side down, into dough to resemble various dominos. Repeat with remaining dough, scraps and chocolate chips.

5. Bake 8 to 10 minutes or until edges are light golden brown. Remove to wire racks; cool completely. *makes 3 dozen cookies*

tip: Use these adorable cookies as a learning tool for kids. They can count the number of chocolate chips in each cookie and arrange them in lots of ways: highest to lowest, numerically or even solve simple math problems. As a treat, they can eat the cookies afterwards.

chocolate syrup brownies

1 egg
1 cup packed light
  brown sugar
¾ cup HERSHEY'S
  Syrup
1½ cups all-purpose flour
¼ teaspoon baking soda
  Dash salt
½ cup (1 stick) butter or
  margarine, melted
¾ cup chopped pecans
  or walnuts

1. Heat oven to 350°F. Grease 9-inch square baking pan.

2. Beat egg lightly in small bowl; add brown sugar and syrup, beating until well blended. Stir together flour, baking soda and salt; gradually add to egg mixture, beating until blended. Stir in butter and nuts. Spread batter into prepared pan.

3. Bake 35 to 40 minutes or until brownies begin to pull away from sides of pan. Cool completely in pan on wire rack. Cut into squares.
makes about 16 brownies

lollipop clowns

1 package (18 ounces) refrigerated red, green or blue cookie dough*

All-purpose flour (optional)

Assorted colored icings and hard candies

SUPPLIES

18 (4-inch) lollipop sticks

*If colored dough in unavailable, sugar cookie dough can be tinted with paste food coloring.

1. Preheat oven to 350°F.

2. Remove dough from wrapper according to package directions. Divide dough into 2 equal sections. Reserve 1 section; cover and refrigerate remaining section.

3. Roll reserved dough on lightly floured surface to ⅛-inch thickness. Sprinkle with flour to minimize sticking, if necessary.

4. Cut out cookies using 3½-inch round cookie cutter. Place lollipop sticks on cookies so that tips of sticks are imbedded in cookies. Carefully turn cookies so sticks are in back; place on ungreased cookie sheets.

5. Bake 8 to 10 minutes or until firm but not brown. Cool on cookie sheets 2 minutes. Remove to wire racks; cool completely.

6. Decorate cookies with icings as shown in photo.

makes about 18 cookies

tip: These happy clown faces make the perfect topping for a birthday cake. Stick a Lollipop Clown, one for each child, in the cake for a wonderful circus theme party.

peanut butter s'mores

- 1½ cups all-purpose flour
- ½ teaspoon baking powder
- ½ teaspoon baking soda
- ¼ teaspoon salt
- ½ cup butter, softened
- ½ cup granulated sugar
- ½ cup packed brown sugar
- ½ cup creamy or chunky peanut butter
- 1 egg
- 1 teaspoon vanilla
- ½ cup chopped roasted peanuts (optional)
- 4 (1.55-ounce) milk chocolate candy bars
- 16 large marshmallows

1. Preheat oven to 350°F.

2. Combine flour, baking powder, baking soda and salt in small bowl; set aside. Beat butter, granulated sugar and brown sugar in large bowl with electric mixer at medium speed until light and fluffy. Beat in peanut butter, egg and vanilla until well blended. Gradually beat in flour mixture at low speed until blended. Stir in peanuts, if desired.

3. Roll dough into 1-inch balls; place 2 inches apart on ungreased cookie sheets. Flatten dough with tines of fork, forming criss-cross pattern. Bake about 14 minutes or until set and edges are light golden brown. Cool cookies 2 minutes on cookie sheets; transfer to wire cooling racks. Cool completely.

4. To assemble sandwiches, break each candy bar into four sections. Place 1 section of chocolate on flat side of 1 cookie. Place on microwavable plate; top with 1 marshmallow. Microwave at HIGH 10 to 12 seconds or until marshmallow is puffy. Immediately top with another cookie, flat side down. Press slightly on top cookie, spreading marshmallow to edges. Repeat with remaining cookies, marshmallows and candy pieces, one at a time. Cool completely.

makes about 16 sandwich cookies

easy peanut butter cookies

1 (14-ounce) can
  EAGLE® BRAND
  Sweetened
  Condensed Milk
  (NOT evaporated
  milk)
¾ to 1 cup peanut butter
1 egg
1 teaspoon vanilla
  extract
2 cups biscuit baking
  mix
  Sugar

1. In large bowl, beat Eagle Brand, peanut butter, egg and vanilla until smooth. Add biscuit mix; mix well. Chill at least 1 hour.

2. Preheat oven to 350°F. Shape dough into 1-inch balls. Roll in sugar. Place 2 inches apart on ungreased baking sheets.

3. Flatten with fork in criss-cross pattern. Bake 6 to 8 minutes or until lightly browned (do not overbake). Cool. Store tightly covered at room temperature.   *makes about 5 dozen*

peanut blossom cookies: Make dough as directed above. Shape into 1-inch balls and roll in sugar; do not flatten. Bake as directed above. Immediately after baking, press solid milk chocolate candy drop in center of each cookie.

peanut butter & jelly gems: Make dough as directed above. Shape into 1-inch balls and roll in sugar; do not flatten. Press thumb in center of each ball of dough; fill with jelly, jam or preserves. Proceed as directed above.

any-way-you-like 'em cookies: Stir 1 cup semi-sweet chocolate chips, chopped peanuts, raisins or flaked coconut into dough. Proceed as directed above.

prep time: 10 minutes
chill time: 1 hour
bake time: 6 to 8 minutes

colorful caramel bites

1 cup plus 6 tablespoons all-purpose flour, divided

1 cup quick-cooking or old-fashioned oats, uncooked

¾ cup firmly packed light brown sugar

½ teaspoon baking soda

¼ teaspoon salt

¾ cup (1½ sticks) butter or margarine, melted

1¾ cups "M&M's"® Semi-Sweet Chocolate Mini Baking Bits, divided

1½ cups chopped pecans, divided

1 jar (12 ounces) caramel ice cream topping

Preheat oven to 350°F. Combine 1 cup flour, oats, sugar, baking soda and salt; blend in melted butter to form crumbly mixture. Press half the crumb mixture onto bottom of 9×9×2-inch baking pan; bake 10 minutes. Sprinkle with 1 cup "M&M's"® Semi-Sweet Chocolate Mini Baking Bits and 1 cup nuts. Blend remaining 6 tablespoons flour with caramel topping; pour over top. Combine remaining crumb mixture, remaining ¾ cup "M&M's"® Semi-Sweet Chocolate Mini Baking Bits and remaining ½ cup nuts; sprinkle over caramel layer. Bake 20 to 25 minutes or until golden brown. Cool completely. Cut into squares.

makes 36 bars

Old-fashioned and quick-cooking oats can usually be used interchangeably in baking recipes. Old-fashioned oats have been steamed and then flattened into flakes, while quick-cooking oats have been cut into pieces before being steamed and flattened. Instant oats *cannot* be used as a substitute.

no-bake fudgy brownies

1 (14-ounce) can EAGLE® BRAND Sweetened Condensed Milk (NOT evaporated milk)

2 (1-ounce) squares unsweetened chocolate, cut up

1 teaspoon vanilla extract

2 cups plus 2 tablespoons packaged chocolate cookie crumbs

¼ cup miniature candy-coated milk chocolate candies or chopped nuts

1. Grease 8-inch square baking pan or line with foil; set aside.

2. In medium-sized heavy saucepan, combine Eagle Brand and chocolate; cook and stir over low heat just until boiling. Reduce heat; cook and stir for 2 to 3 minutes more or until mixture thickens. Remove from heat. Stir in vanilla.

3. Stir in 2 cups cookie crumbs. Spread evenly in prepared pan. Sprinkle with remaining cookie crumbs and candies or nuts; press down gently with back of spoon.

4. Cover and chill 4 hours or until firm. Cut into squares. Store covered in refrigerator.
makes 24 to 36 bars

prep time: 10 minutes
chill time: 4 hours

sunshine butter cookies

¾ cup butter, softened

¾ cup sugar

1 egg

2¼ cups all-purpose flour

¼ teaspoon salt

Grated peel of
½ lemon

1 teaspoon frozen
lemonade
concentrate, thawed

Lemonade Royal Icing
(recipe follows)

Thin pretzel sticks

Yellow paste food
color

Gummy fruit and
black licorice
strings

1. Beat butter and sugar in large bowl at high speed of electric mixer until fluffy. Add egg; beat well.

2. Combine flour, salt and lemon peel in medium bowl. Add to butter mixture. Stir in lemonade concentrate. Refrigerate 2 hours.

3. Prepare Lemonade Royal Icing. Cover; let stand at room temperature. Preheat oven to 350°F. Grease cookie sheets.

4. Roll dough on floured surface to ⅛-inch thickness. Cut out cookies using 3-inch round cookie cutter. Place cookies on prepared cookie sheets. Press pretzel sticks into edges of cookies to resemble sunshine rays; press gently. Bake 10 minutes or until lightly browned. Remove to wire racks; cool completely.

5. Add food color to Lemonade Royal Icing. Spoon about ½ cup icing into resealable plastic food storage bag; seal. Cut tiny tip from corner of bag. Pipe thin circle around flat side of each cookie to create outline.

6. Add water, 1 tablespoon at a time, to remaining icing in bowl until thick but pourable consistency. Spoon icing in cookie centers staying within outline.

7. Decorate cookies with gummy fruit and licorice to make "sunny" faces. Let stand 1 hour or until dry.   *makes about 3 dozen cookies*

Lemonade Royal Icing: Beat 3¾ cups sifted powdered sugar, 3 tablespoons meringue powder and 6 tablespoons frozen lemonade concentrate, thawed, in large bowl of electric mixer until smooth. (Meringue powder is available in stores that carry cake decorating supplies.)

child's choice

2⅓ cups all-purpose flour

1 Butter Flavor CRISCO® Stick or 1 cup Butter Flavor CRISCO® all-vegetable shortening plus additional for greasing

1 teaspoon baking soda

½ teaspoon baking powder

1 cup granulated sugar

1 cup firmly packed brown sugar

2 eggs

1 teaspoon maple flavor

2 cups oats (quick or old fashioned, uncooked)

¾ cup semi-sweet chocolate chips

¾ cup miniature marshmallows

¾ cup peanut butter chips

1. Heat oven to 350°F. Grease baking sheet with shortening. Place sheets of foil on countertop for cooling cookies.

2. Combine flour, 1 cup shortening, baking soda and baking powder in large bowl. Beat at low speed of electric mixer until blended. Increase speed to medium. Mix thoroughly. Beat in granulated sugar, brown sugar, eggs and maple flavor. Add oats. Stir in chocolate chips, marshmallows and peanut butter chips with spoon until well blended.

3. Shape dough into 1½-inch balls. Flatten slightly. Place 2 inches apart on prepared baking sheet.

4. Bake at 350°F for 9 to 10 minutes or until light golden brown. *Do not overbake.* Cool 2 minutes on baking sheet. Remove cookies to foil to cool completely.   *makes about 3½ dozen cookies*

After the first batch of cookies are done, allow the baking sheet to cool to room temperature before adding more cookie dough. If the baking sheet is too hot, it will cause the dough to melt and spread, changing the texture and shape of the cookies.

248

buckeye cookie bars

1 (18¼-ounce) package chocolate cake mix

¼ cup vegetable oil

1 egg

1 cup chopped peanuts

1 (14-ounce) can EAGLE® BRAND Sweetened Condensed Milk (NOT evaporated milk)

½ cup peanut butter

1. Preheat oven to 350°F.

2. In large mixing bowl, combine cake mix, oil and egg; beat on medium speed until crumbly. Stir in peanuts. Reserving 1½ cups crumb mixture, press remainder firmly on bottom of greased 13×9 inch baking pan.

3. In medium bowl, beat Eagle Brand with peanut butter until smooth; spread over prepared crust. Sprinkle with reserved crumb mixture.

4. Bake 25 to 30 minutes or until set. Cool. Cut into bars. Store loosely covered at room temperature. *makes 24 to 36 bars*

prep time: 20 minutes
bake time: 25 to 30 minutes

candy shop pizza

1 package (18 ounces) NESTLÉ® TOLL HOUSE® Refrigerated Chocolate Chip Cookie Bar Dough

1 cup (6 ounces) NESTLÉ® TOLL HOUSE® Semi-Sweet Chocolate Morsels

½ cup creamy or chunky peanut butter

1 cup coarsely chopped assorted NESTLÉ® candy such as Butterfinger® bars, Crunch® bars, Baby Ruth® bars, Goobers® or Raisinets®

Preheat oven to 325°F. Grease baking sheet or pizza pan.

Place whole bar of dough scored side down onto prepared baking sheet or pizza pan.

Bake for 30 to 35 minutes or until golden brown. Immediately sprinkle morsels over hot crust; drop peanut butter by spoonfuls onto morsels. Let stand for 5 minutes or until morsels become shiny and soft. Gently spread chocolate and peanut butter evenly over cookie crust.

Sprinkle candy in single layer over pizza. Cut into wedges; serve warm or at room temperature. *makes about 12 servings*

variation: Substitute 1 package (18 ounces) NESTLÉ® TOLL HOUSE® Refrigerated Sugar Cookie Bar Dough. Press cookie dough onto greased large baking sheet or pizza pan to measure an 8-inch circle. Bake for 16 to 18 minutes or until lightly golden.

happy face oatmeal monsters

1½ cups all-purpose flour

1 teaspoon baking soda

½ teaspoon salt

1 cup butter, softened

1 cup packed brown sugar

2 eggs

1 teaspoon vanilla

2 cups uncooked quick oats

Granulated sugar

28 chocolate-covered candies or large chocolate chips

Cinnamon red hot candies or red licorice strings

Colored frosting in tube and flaked coconut (optional)

1. Preheat oven to 350°F.

2. Combine flour, baking soda and salt in small bowl; set aside. Beat butter and brown sugar in large bowl of electric mixer at medium speed until light and fluffy. Beat in eggs, one at a time, until well blended. Beat in vanilla. Gradually beat in flour mixture on low speed until blended. Stir in oats.

3. Drop dough by level ¼ cupfuls onto ungreased cookie sheets, spacing 3 inches apart. Flatten dough until 2 inches in diameter with bottom of glass that has been dipped in granulated sugar. Press chocolate candies into cookies to form "eyes" and use cinnamon candies or licorice for "mouth."

4. Bake 12 to 14 minutes or until cookies are set and edges are golden brown. Cool cookies 2 minutes on cookie sheets; transfer to wire racks. Cool completely.

5. If desired, decorate cookies with frosting and coconut to form "hair."

makes about 14 (4-inch) cookies

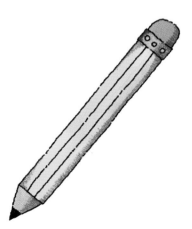

candy bar bars

¾ cup (1½ sticks) butter or margarine, softened

¼ cup peanut butter

1 cup packed brown sugar

1 teaspoon baking soda

2 cups quick-cooking oats

1½ cups all-purpose flour

1 egg

1 (14-ounce) can EAGLE® BRAND Sweetened Condensed Milk (NOT evaporated milk)

4 cups chopped candy bars (such as chocolate-coated caramel-topped nougat bars with peanuts, chocolate-covered crisp wafers, chocolate-covered caramel-topped cookie bars, or chocolate-covered peanut butter cups)

1. Preheat oven to 350°F. In large bowl, combine butter and peanut butter. Add sugar and baking soda; beat well. Stir in oats and flour. Reserve 1¾ cups crumb mixture.

2. Stir egg into remaining crumb mixture; press firmly on bottom of ungreased 15×10×1-inch baking pan. Bake 15 minutes.

3. Spread Eagle Brand over baked crust. Stir together reserved crumb mixture and candy bar pieces; sprinkle evenly over top. Bake 25 minutes or until golden. Cool. Cut into bars. Store covered at room temperature. *makes 48 bars*

prep time: 20 minutes
bake time: 40 minutes

To soften butter quickly and easily, place 1 stick of butter on a microwave-safe plate and heat at LOW (30% power) about 30 seconds or just until softened.

252

candy bar bars

cheery chocolate animal cookies

1⅔ cups (10-ounce package) REESE'S® Peanut Butter Chips

1 cup HERSHEY'S® Semi-Sweet Chocolate Chips

2 tablespoons shortening (do not use butter, margarine, spread or oil)

1 package (20 ounces) chocolate sandwich cookies

1 package (11 ounces) animal crackers

1. Line trays or cookie sheets with wax paper.

2. Combine peanut butter chips, chocolate chips and shortening in 2-quart glass measuring cup with handle. Microwave on HIGH (100% power) 1½ to 2 minutes or until chips are melted and mixture is smooth when stirred. Using fork, dip each cookie into melted chip mixture; gently tap fork on side of cup to remove excess chocolate.

3. Place coated cookies on prepared trays; top each cookie with an animal cracker. Chill until chocolate is set, about 30 minutes. Store in airtight container in a cool, dry place.

makes about 4 dozen cookies

philadelphia® snowmen cookies

1 package (8 ounces) PHILADELPHIA® Cream Cheese, softened

1 cup powdered sugar

¾ cup (1½ sticks) butter *or* margarine

½ teaspoon vanilla

2¼ cups flour

½ teaspoon baking soda

Sifted powdered sugar

Miniature peanut butter cups (optional)

MIX cream cheese, 1 cup sugar, butter and vanilla with electric mixer on medium speed until well blended. Add flour and baking soda; mix well.

SHAPE dough into equal number of ½-inch and 1-inch diameter balls. Using 1 small and 1 large ball for each snowman, place balls, slightly overlapping, on ungreased cookie sheets. Flatten to ¼-inch thickness with bottom of glass dipped in additional flour. Repeat with remaining balls.

BAKE at 325°F for 19 to 21 minutes or until light golden brown. Cool on wire racks. Sprinkle each snowman with sifted powdered sugar. Decorate with icing as desired. Cut peanut butter cups in half for hats.

makes about 3 dozen cookies

prep time: 20 minutes
bake time: 21 minutes

254

chocolate cream cheese sugar cookie bars

1 package (22.3 ounces) golden sugar cookie mix

3 eggs, divided

⅓ cup plus 6 tablespoons butter or margarine, softened and divided

1 teaspoon water

1 package (8 ounces) cream cheese, softened

1 package (3 ounces) cream cheese, softened

¾ cup granulated sugar

⅓ cup HERSHEY'S Cocoa

1½ teaspoons vanilla extract

Powdered sugar

1. Heat oven to 350°F.

2. Empty cookie mix into large bowl. Break up any lumps. Add 2 eggs, ⅓ cup butter and water; stir with spoon or fork until well blended. Spread into ungreased 13×9×2-inch baking pan.

3. Beat cream cheese and remaining 6 tablespoons butter in medium bowl on medium speed of mixer until fluffy. Stir together granulated sugar and cocoa; gradually add to cream cheese mixture, beating until smooth and well blended. Add remaining egg and vanilla; beat well. Spread cream cheese mixture evenly over cookie batter.

4. Bake 35 to 40 minutes or until no imprint remains when touched lightly in center. Cool completely in pan on wire rack. Sprinkle powdered sugar over top. Cut into bars. Cover; store leftover bars in refrigerator.

makes about 24 to 30 bars

To soften cream cheese for recipes, remove it from the wrapper and place in a medium microwave-safe bowl. Microwave on MEDIUM (50% power) 15 to 20 seconds or until slightly softened.

256

peanut butter & jelly streusel bars

1¼ cups firmly packed light brown sugar

¾ cup creamy peanut butter

½ CRISCO® Stick or ½ cup CRISCO® all-vegetable shortening plus additional for greasing

3 tablespoons milk

1 tablespoon vanilla

1 egg

1¾ cups all-purpose flour

¾ teaspoon baking soda

¾ teaspoon salt

1 cup strawberry jam, stirred

½ cup quick oats, uncooked

1. Heat oven to 350°F. Grease 13×9-inch baking pan. Place cooling rack on countertop.

2. Place brown sugar, peanut butter, shortening, milk and vanilla in large bowl. Beat at medium speed of electric mixer until well blended. Add egg; beat just until blended.

3. Combine flour, baking soda and salt. Add to shortening mixture; beat at low speed just until blended.

4. Press ⅔ of dough onto bottom of prepared baking pan. Spread jam over dough to within ¼ inch of edges.

5. Add oats to remaining dough. Drop dough by spoonfuls onto jam.

6. Bake at 350°F for 20 to 25 minutes or until edges and streusel topping are lightly browned. *Do not overbake.* Cool completely on cooling rack. Cut into 2×1½-inch bars.   *makes about 3 dozen bars*

quick peanut butter chocolate chip cookies

1 package DUNCAN HINES® Moist Deluxe® Classic Yellow Cake Mix

½ cup creamy peanut butter

½ cup butter or margarine, softened

2 eggs

1 cup milk chocolate chips

1. Preheat oven to 350°F. Grease cookie sheets.

2. Combine cake mix, peanut butter, butter and eggs in large bowl. Mix at low speed with electric mixer until blended. Stir in chocolate chips.

3. Drop by rounded teaspoonfuls onto prepared cookie sheets. Bake 9 to 11 minutes or until lightly browned. Cool 2 minutes on cookie sheets. Remove to cooling racks.   *makes about 4 dozen cookies*

tip: Crunchy peanut butter may be substituted for regular peanut butter.

circus cookies

2 cups all-purpose flour

½ teaspoon baking powder

¼ teaspoon salt

1 cup margarine, softened

½ cup granulated sugar

2 eggs

½ cup orange juice

2 cups KELLOGG'S® FROOT LOOPS® cereal, crushed to fine crumbs

ORANGE ICING

2 cups confectioners sugar

3 tablespoons margarine, softened

2 tablespoons orange juice

1. Preheat oven to 350°F. Stir together flour, baking powder and salt. Set aside.

2. In large mixing bowl, beat 1 cup margarine and granulated sugar until light and fluffy. Add eggs and ½ cup orange juice. Beat well. Add flour mixture. Mix until well combined. Stir in Kellogg's® Froot Loops® cereal. Drop by level measuring tablespoonfuls, about two inches apart, onto ungreased cookie sheets.

3. Bake about 12 minutes or until lightly browned. Remove immediately from cookie sheets. Cool on wire racks.

4. To make Orange Icing, measure confectioners sugar, margarine and orange juice in small mixing bowl. Beat until smooth. When cookies are completely cooled, frost and decorate with additional cereal, whole or crushed.

makes about 4 dozen cookies

peanut butter and chocolate spirals

1 package (20 ounces) refrigerated sugar cookie dough

1 package (20 ounces) refrigerated peanut butter cookie dough

¼ cup unsweetened cocoa powder

⅓ cup peanut butter-flavored chips, chopped

¼ cup all-purpose flour

⅓ cup miniature chocolate chips

1. Remove each dough from wrapper according to package directions.

2. Place sugar cookie dough and cocoa in large bowl; mix with fork to blend. Stir in peanut butter chips.

3. Place peanut butter cookie dough and flour in another large bowl; mix with fork to blend. Stir in chocolate chips. Divide each dough in half; cover and refrigerate 1 hour.

4. Roll each dough on floured surface to 12×6-inch rectangle. Layer each half of peanut butter dough onto each half of chocolate dough. Roll up doughs, starting at long end to form 2 (12-inch) rolls. Wrap in plastic wrap; refrigerate 1 hour.

5. Preheat oven to 375°F. Cut dough into ½-inch-thick slices. Place cookies 2 inches apart on ungreased cookie sheets.

6. Bake 10 to 12 minutes or until lightly browned. Remove to wire racks; cool completely. *makes 4 dozen cookies*

cheery chocolate teddy bear cookies

1⅔ cups (10-ounce) package REESE'S® Peanut Butter Chips

1 cup HERSHEY'S® Semi-Sweet Chocolate Chips

2 tablespoons shortening (do *not* use butter, margarine, spread or oil)

1 package (20 ounces) chocolate sandwich cookies

1 package (10 ounces) teddy bear shaped graham snack crackers

1. Line tray or cookie sheet with wax paper.

2. Combine chips and shortening in 2-quart glass measuring cup with handle. Microwave on HIGH (100% power) 1½ to 2 minutes or until chips are melted and mixture is smooth when stirred. Using fork, dip each cookie into chip mixture; gently tap fork on side of cup to remove excess chocolate.

3. Place coated cookies on prepared tray; top each cookie with one graham snack cracker. Chill until chocolate is set, about 30 minutes. Store in airtight container in a cool, dry place.

makes about 4 dozen cookies

260

critters-in-holes

48 chewy caramel candies coated in milk chocolate

48 pieces candy corn

Miniature candy-coated chocolate pieces

1 container (16 ounces) frosting, any flavor

1 package (20 ounces) refrigerated peanut butter cookie dough

1. Cut slit into side of 1 caramel candy using sharp knife. Carefully insert 1 piece candy corn into slit. Repeat with remaining caramel candies and candy corn.

2. Attach miniature chocolate pieces to caramel candies to resemble eyes, using frosting as glue. Decorate as desired.

3. Preheat oven to 350°F. Grease 12 (1¾-inch) muffin cups.

4. Remove dough from wrapper according to package directions. Cut dough into 12 (1-inch) slices. Cut each slice into 4 equal sections. Place 1 section of dough into each muffin cup.

5. Bake 9 minutes. Remove from oven and immediately press 1 decorated caramel candy into center of each cookie. Repeat with remaining candies and cookies. Remove to wire racks; cool completely.

makes 4 dozen cookies

baker's® one bowl super chunk cookies

1 package (8 squares) BAKER'S® Semi-Sweet Baking Chocolate

½ cup (1 stick) butter *or* margarine

½ cup granulated sugar

½ cup firmly packed brown sugar

1 egg

1 teaspoon vanilla

1 cup flour

1 cup quick-cooking rolled oats

½ teaspoon baking soda

½ cup chopped nuts (optional)

HEAT oven to 375°F. Break chocolate squares in half; cut each half into 3 chunks.

BEAT butter, sugars, egg and vanilla in large bowl with electric mixer on medium speed 1 minute or until well blended. Beat in flour, oats and baking soda on low speed until combined. Stir in chocolate and nuts.

DROP by rounded tablespoonfuls onto ungreased cookie sheet.

BAKE 10 minutes or until lightly browned. Cool on cookie sheet 2 minutes. Cool completely on wire rack.

makes about 2 dozen cookies

variation: Prepare as directed, substituting 1 cup lightly toasted Baker's® Angel Flake® Coconut for the nuts.

prep time: 10 minutes
bake time: 10 minutes

262

peanut butter crackles

1½ **cups all-purpose flour**

1 **teaspoon baking soda**

⅛ **teaspoon salt**

½ **cup (1 stick) margarine or butter, softened**

½ **cup SKIPPY® Creamy or SUPER CHUNK® Peanut Butter**

½ **cup granulated sugar**

½ **cup packed brown sugar**

1 **egg**

1 **teaspoon vanilla**

Granulated sugar

Chocolate candy kisses

1. Preheat oven at 375°F. In small bowl, combine flour, baking soda and salt; set aside.

2. In large bowl, beat margarine and peanut butter until smooth. Beat in sugars until blended. Beat in egg and vanilla. Gradually beat in flour mixture until well mixed.

3. Shape dough into 1-inch balls. Roll in granulated sugar. Place 2 inches apart on ungreased cookie sheets.

4. Bake 10 minutes or until lightly browned. Remove from oven and quickly press chocolate candy kiss firmly into top of each cookie (cookie will crack around edges). Remove to wire racks to cool completely. *makes about 5 dozen cookies*

cookie pops

1 **package (20 ounces) refrigerated sugar cookie dough**

All-purpose flour (optional)

20 **(4-inch) lollipop sticks**

Assorted frostings, glazes and decors

1. Preheat oven to 350°F. Grease cookie sheets.

2. Remove dough from wrapper according to package directions. Sprinkle with flour to minimize sticking, if necessary.

3. Cut dough in half. Reserve 1 half; refrigerate remaining dough. Roll reserved dough to ⅛-inch thickness. Cut out cookies using 3½-inch cookie cutters.

4. Place lollipop sticks on cookies so that tips of sticks are imbedded in cookies. Carefully turn cookies so sticks are in back; place on prepared cookie sheets. Repeat with remaining dough.

5. Bake 7 to 11 minutes or until edges are lightly browned. Cool cookies on cookie sheets 2 minutes. Remove cookies to wire racks; cool completely.

6. Decorate with frostings, glazes and decors as desired. *makes 20 cookies*

COOKIES

chocolate drop sugar cookies

⅔ cup butter or
    margarine, softened

1 cup sugar

1 egg

1½ teaspoons vanilla
    extract

1½ cups all-purpose flour

½ cup HERSHEY'S
    Cocoa

½ teaspoon baking soda

¼ teaspoon salt

⅓ cup buttermilk or sour
    milk*

Additional sugar

*To sour milk: Use 1 teaspoon
white vinegar plus milk to equal
⅓ cup.

1. Heat oven to 350°F. Lightly grease cookie sheet.

2. Beat butter and sugar in large bowl until well blended. Add egg and vanilla; beat until fluffy. Stir together flour, cocoa, baking soda and salt; add alternately with buttermilk to butter mixture. Using ice cream scoop or ¼-cup measuring cup, drop dough about 2 inches apart onto prepared cookie sheet.

3. Bake 13 to 15 minutes or until cookie springs back when touched lightly in center. While cookies are on cookie sheet, sprinkle lightly with additional sugar. Cool slightly; remove from cookie sheet to wire rack. Cool completely.   *makes about 1 dozen cookies*

philadelphia® cheesecake brownies

1 package (19.8 ounces)
    brownie mix
    (do not use mix
    that includes syrup
    pouch)

1 package (8 ounces)
    PHILADELPHIA®
    Cream Cheese,
    softened

⅓ cup sugar

1 egg

½ teaspoon vanilla

PREPARE brownie mix as directed on package. Pour into greased 13×9-inch baking pan.

BEAT cream cheese with electric mixer on medium speed until smooth. Mix in sugar until blended. Add egg and vanilla; mix just until blended. Pour cream cheese mixture over brownie batter; cut through batter with knife several times for marble effect.

BAKE at 350°F for 35 to 40 minutes or until cream cheese mixture is lightly browned. Cool. Cut into squares.   *makes 2 dozen*

special extras: For extra chocolate flavor, sprinkle 1 cup BAKER'S® Semi-Sweet Real Chocolate Chips over top of brownies before baking.

prep time: 20 minutes
bake time: 40 minutes

265

DESSERTS

clown-around cones

4 waffle cones

½ cup "M&M's"® Chocolate Mini Baking Bits, divided

Prepared decorator icing

½ cup hot fudge ice cream topping, divided

4 cups any flavor ice cream, softened

1 (1.5- to 2-ounce) chocolate candy bar, chopped

¼ cup caramel ice cream topping

Decorate cones as desired with "M&M's"® Chocolate Mini Baking Bits, using decorator icing to attach; let set. For each cone, place 1 tablespoon hot fudge topping in bottom of cone. Sprinkle with 1 teaspoon "M&M's"® Chocolate Mini Baking Bits. Layer with ¼ cup ice cream; sprinkle with ¼ of candy bar. Layer with ¼ cup ice cream; sprinkle with 1 teaspoon "M&M's"® Chocolate Mini Baking Bits. Top with 1 tablespoon caramel topping and remaining ½ cup ice cream. Wrap in plastic wrap and freeze until ready to serve. Just before serving, top each ice cream cone with 1 tablespoon hot fudge topping; sprinkle with remaining "M&M's"® Chocolate Mini Baking Bits. Serve immediately.

makes 4 servings

brownie ice cream pie

1 package DUNCAN
HINES® Chewy
Fudge Brownie Mix

2 eggs

½ cup vegetable oil

¼ cup water

¾ cup semisweet
chocolate chips

1 (9-inch) unbaked
pastry crust

1 (10-ounce) package
frozen sweetened
sliced strawberries

Vanilla ice cream

Preheat oven to 350°F.

Combine brownie mix, eggs, oil and water in large bowl. Stir with spoon until well blended, about 50 strokes. Stir in chips. Spoon into crust. Bake 40 to 45 minutes or until set. Cool completely. Purée strawberries in food processor or blender. Cut pie into wedges. Serve with ice cream and puréed strawberries. *makes 8 servings*

gelatin poke cake

1 package (2-layer size)
white cake mix or
cake mix with
pudding in the mix

1 cup boiling water

1 package (4-serving
size) JELL-O® Brand
Gelatin Dessert, any
flavor

½ cup cold water

1 tub (8 ounces) COOL
WHIP® Whipped
Topping, thawed

HEAT oven to 350°F.

PREPARE and bake cake mix as directed on package for 13×9-inch baking pan. Remove from oven. Cool cake in pan 15 minutes. Pierce cake with large fork at ½-inch intervals.

MEANWHILE, stir boiling water into gelatin in medium bowl at least 2 minutes until completely dissolved. Stir in cold water; carefully pour over cake. Refrigerate 3 hours.

FROST with whipped topping. Refrigerate at least 1 hour or until ready to serve. Decorate as desired. *makes 15 servings*

preparation time: 15 minutes
baking time: 35 minutes
refrigerating time: 4 hours

hot fudge pudding cake

1¼ cups granulated sugar, divided

1 cup all-purpose flour

½ cup HERSHEY'S Cocoa, divided

2 teaspoons baking powder

¼ teaspoon salt

½ cup milk

⅓ cup butter or margarine, melted

1½ teaspoons vanilla extract

½ cup packed light brown sugar

1¼ cups hot water

Whipped topping

1. Heat oven to 350°F.

2. Stir together ¾ cup granulated sugar, flour, ¼ cup cocoa, baking powder and salt. Stir in milk, butter and vanilla; beat until smooth. Pour batter into ungreased 9-inch square baking pan. Stir together remaining ½ cup granulated sugar, brown sugar and remaining ¼ cup cocoa; sprinkle mixture evenly over batter. Pour hot water over top. Do not stir.

3. Bake 35 to 40 minutes or until center is almost set. Let stand 15 minutes; spoon into dessert dishes, spooning sauce from bottom of pan over top. Garnish with whipped topping.

makes about 8 servings

prep time: 10 minutes
bake time: 35 minutes
cool time: 15 minutes

cherry-berry crumble

1 (21-ounce) can cherry pie filling

2 cups fresh or frozen raspberries

1 (14-ounce) can EAGLE® BRAND Sweetened Condensed Milk (NOT evaporated milk)

1½ cups granola

1. In medium-sized saucepan, cook and stir cherry pie filling and raspberries until heated through. Stir in Eagle Brand; cook and stir for 1 minute more.

2. Spoon into 2-quart square baking dish or into 6 individual dessert dishes. Sprinkle with granola. Serve warm.   *makes 6 servings*

peach-berry crumble: Substitute peach pie filling for cherry pie filling.

cherry-rhubarb crumble: Substitute fresh or frozen sliced rhubarb for the raspberries. In medium-sized saucepan, cook and stir pie filling and rhubarb until bubbly. Cook and stir 5 minutes more. Proceed as above.

prep time: 10 minutes

oreo® cheesecake

1 (1-pound 4-ounce)
   package OREO®
   Chocolate Sandwich
   Cookies, divided

⅓ cup margarine or
   butter, melted

3 (8-ounce) packages
   cream cheese,
   softened

¾ cup sugar

4 eggs

1 cup sour cream

1 teaspoon vanilla
   extract

   Whipped cream and
   mint sprigs, for
   garnish

   Additional OREO®
   Chocolate Sandwich
   Cookies, halved, for
   garnish

1. Finely crush 30 cookies and coarsely chop 20 cookies; set aside. Mix finely crushed cookie crumbs and margarine or butter in bowl. Press on bottom and 2 inches up side of 9-inch springform pan; set aside.

2. Beat cream cheese and sugar in medium bowl with electric mixer at medium speed until creamy. Blend in eggs, sour cream and vanilla; fold in chopped cookies. Spread mixture into prepared crust. Bake at 350°F for 55 to 60 minutes or until set. (If necessary to prevent top from overbrowning, tent with foil for the last 15 to 20 minutes of baking.)

3. Cool on wire rack at room temperature. Refrigerate at least 4 hours.

4. Remove side of pan; garnish with whipped cream, mint sprigs and cookie halves to serve. *makes 16 servings*

preparation time: 25 minutes
cook time: 55 minutes
cooling time: 1 hour
chill time: 4 hours
total time: 6 hours and 20 minutes

To finely crush Oreo® cookies, seal them in a large plastic bag, then go over them with a rolling pin until they are about the size of cornmeal. To chop Oreo® cookies, use a sharp knife to cut the cookies into small uniform pieces.

wild side sundaes

4 packages (4-serving size) JELL-O® Brand Gelatin, 4 different flavors

4 cups boiling water

2 cups cold water

1 tub (8 ounces) COOL WHIP® Whipped Topping, thawed

Additional thawed COOL WHIP® Whipped Topping

DISSOLVE each package of gelatin completely in 1 cup boiling water in separate bowls. Stir ½ cup cold water into each bowl of gelatin. Pour each mixture into separate 8-inch square pans. Refrigerate at least 3 hours or until firm. Cut gelatin in each pan into ½-inch cubes.

LAYER gelatin cubes alternately with whipped topping in sundae glasses. Garnish with dollop of additional whipped topping.

REFRIGERATE until ready to serve.   *makes 16 servings*

chocolate syrup swirl cake

1 cup (2 sticks) butter or margarine, softened

2 cups sugar

2 teaspoons vanilla extract

3 eggs

2¾ cups all-purpose flour

1¼ teaspoons baking soda, divided

½ teaspoon salt

1 cup buttermilk or sour milk*

1 cup HERSHEY'S Syrup

1 cup MOUNDS® Sweetened Coconut Flakes (optional)

To sour milk: Use 1 tablespoon white vinegar plus milk to equal 1 cup.

1. Heat oven to 350°F. Grease and flour 12-cup fluted tube pan or 10-inch tube pan.

2. Beat butter, sugar and vanilla in large bowl until fluffy. Add eggs; beat well. Stir together flour, 1 teaspoon baking soda and salt; add alternately with buttermilk to butter mixture, beating until well blended.

3. Measure 2 cups batter in small bowl; stir in syrup and remaining ¼ teaspoon baking soda. Add coconut, if desired, to remaining batter; pour into prepared pan. Pour chocolate batter over vanilla batter in pan; do not mix.

4. Bake 60 to 70 minutes or until wooden pick inserted in center comes out clean. Cool 15 minutes; remove from pan to wire rack. Cool completely on wire rack; glaze or frost as desired.

makes 20 servings

fudge ribbon sheet cake

1 (18¼-ounce) package chocolate cake mix

1 (8-ounce) package cream cheese, softened

2 tablespoons butter or margarine, softened

1 tablespoon cornstarch

1 (14-ounce) can EAGLE® BRAND Sweetened Condensed Milk (NOT evaporated milk)

1 egg

1 teaspoon vanilla extract

Chocolate Glaze (recipe follows)

1. Preheat oven to 350°F. Grease and flour 13×9-inch baking pan. Prepare cake mix as package directs. Pour batter into prepared pan.

2. In small bowl, beat cream cheese, butter and cornstarch until fluffy. Gradually beat in Eagle Brand. Add egg and vanilla; beat until smooth. Spoon evenly over cake batter.

3. Bake 40 minutes or until wooden pick inserted near center comes out clean. Cool. Prepare Chocolate Glaze and drizzle over cake. Store covered in refrigerator.   *makes 10 to 12 servings*

chocolate glaze: In small saucepan over low heat, melt 1 (1-ounce) square unsweetened or semi-sweet chocolate and 1 tablespoon butter or margarine with 2 tablespoons water. Remove from heat. Stir in ¾ cup powdered sugar and ½ teaspoon vanilla extract. Stir until smooth and well blended. Makes about ⅓ cup.

fudge ribbon bundt cake: Preheat oven to 350°F. Grease and flour 10-inch bundt pan. Prepare cake mix as package directs. Pour batter into prepared pan. Prepare cream cheese topping as directed above; spoon evenly over batter. Bake 50 to 55 minutes or until wooden pick inserted near center comes out clean. Cool 10 minutes. Remove from pan. Cool. Prepare Chocolate Glaze and drizzle over cake. Store covered in refrigerator.

prep time: 20 minutes
bake time: 40 minutes

276

fudge ribbon sheet cake

original banana pudding

¾ cup sugar, divided

⅓ cup all-purpose flour
   Dash salt

3 eggs, separated

2 cups milk

½ teaspoon vanilla extract

35 NILLA® Wafers

5 bananas, sliced (about 3½ cups)

1. Mix ½ cup sugar, flour and salt in top of double boiler. Blend in 3 egg yolks and milk. Cook, uncovered, over boiling water, stirring constantly 10 to 12 minutes or until thickened. Remove from heat; stir in vanilla.

2. Spread small amount of custard on bottom of 1½-quart round casserole; cover with layer of wafers and layer of sliced bananas. Pour ⅓ of custard over bananas. Continue to layer wafers, bananas and custard to make 3 layers of each, ending with custard.

3. Beat reserved egg whites in small bowl with electric mixer at high speed until soft peaks form; gradually add remaining ¼ cup sugar, beating until mixture forms stiff peaks. Spoon on top of custard, spreading to cover entire surface and sealing well to edges.

4. Bake at 350°F for 15 to 20 minutes or until browned. Garnish with additional banana slices if desired. Serve warm or cold.

makes 8 servings

quick banana pudding: Prepare 2 (4-serving size) packages instant vanilla pudding & pie filling according to package directions. Layer prepared pudding with wafers and bananas as above. Cover; refrigerate at least 3 hours. Garnish with 2 cups prepared whipped topping and additional banana slices.

quick chocolate mousse

1 (14-ounce) can EAGLE® BRAND Sweetened Condensed Milk (NOT evaporated milk)

1 (4-serving size) package chocolate flavor instant pudding mix

1 cup cold water

1 cup (½ pint) whipping cream, whipped

1. In large mixer bowl, beat Eagle Brand, pudding mix and water; chill 5 minutes.

2. Fold in whipped cream. Spoon into serving dishes; chill. Garnish as desired.   *makes 8 to 10 servings*

prep time: 5 minutes

oreo® pizza

14 Regular or Reduced Fat OREO® Chocolate Sandwich Cookies, chopped (about 1½ cups)

1 (21-ounce) package brownie mix, batter prepared according to package directions

1 cup JET-PUFFED® Miniature Marshmallows

⅓ cup PLANTERS® Walnuts, chopped

⅓ cup candy-coated peanut butter candies

1. Stir cookie pieces into prepared brownie batter; spread in greased 14-inch pizza pan. Bake at 350°F for 18 to 20 minutes or until done.

2. Sprinkle marshmallows over top of hot brownie; bake for 2 to 3 minutes more or until marshmallows are puffed.

3. Sprinkle with nuts and candies, pressing lightly into softened marshmallows. Cool slightly on wire rack. Cut into wedges; serve warm or cooled.   *makes 8 servings*

caramel apple cupcakes

1 package butter-recipe yellow cake mix plus ingredients to prepare mix

1 cup chopped dried apples

Caramel Frosting (recipe follows)

Chopped nuts (optional)

1. Preheat oven to 375°F. Line 24 regular-size (2½-inch) muffin pan cups with paper muffin cup liners.

2. Prepare cake mix according to package directions. Stir in apples. Spoon batter into prepared muffin pans.

3. Bake 15 to 20 minutes or until toothpick inserted into centers comes out clean. Cool in pans on wire racks 10 minutes. Remove to racks; cool completely.

4. Prepare Caramel Frosting. Frost cupcakes. Sprinkle cupcakes with nuts, if desired. *makes 24 cupcakes*

caramel frosting: Melt 3 tablespoons butter in medium saucepan. Stir in 1 cup packed brown sugar, ½ cup evaporated milk and ½ teaspoon salt. Bring to a boil, stirring constantly. Remove from heat; cool to lukewarm. Beat in 3¾ cups powdered sugar until frosting is of spreading consistency. Stir in ¾ teaspoon vanilla.

One 14-ounce can of evaporated milk contains 1¾ cups. Unused evaporated milk should be stored in an airtight container in the refrigerator and used within 5 days.

dish of dirt

14 OREO® Chocolate Sandwich Cookies, finely crushed (about 1 cup crumbs), divided

1 pint chocolate ice cream

¼ cup chocolate-flavored syrup

Gummy worms, for garnish

Prepared whipped topping, for garnish

1. In each of 4 dessert dishes, place 2 tablespoons cookie crumbs. Top each with ½ cup ice cream, remaining 2 tablespoons cookie crumbs and 1 tablespoon syrup.

2. Garnish with gummy worms and whipped topping.

makes 4 servings

rocky road pudding

¼ cup sugar

5 tablespoons unsweetened cocoa powder

3 tablespoons cornstarch

⅛ teaspoon salt

2½ cups low-fat (1%) milk

2 egg yolks, beaten

2 teaspoons vanilla

6 packets sugar substitute *or* equivalent of ¼ cup sugar

1 cup miniature marshmallows

¼ cup chopped walnuts, toasted

1. Combine sugar, cocoa, cornstarch and salt in small saucepan; mix well. Stir in milk; cook over medium-high heat, stirring constantly, about 10 minutes or until mixture thickens and begins to boil.

2. Pour about ½ cup pudding mixture over beaten egg yolks in small bowl; beat well. Pour mixture back into saucepan. Cook over medium heat an additional 10 minutes. Remove from heat; stir in vanilla.

3. Place plastic wrap on surface of pudding. Refrigerate about 20 minutes or until slightly cooled. Remove plastic wrap; stir in sugar substitute. Spoon pudding into 6 dessert dishes; top with marshmallows and nuts. Serve warm or cold.

makes 6 servings

282

peanut butter cup cookie ice cream pie

½ cup creamy peanut
   butter
¼ cup honey
1 quart (2 pints) vanilla
   ice cream, softened
1 cup KEEBLER® Chips
   Deluxe™ With
   Peanut Butter Cups
   Cookies, chopped
1 (6-ounce) READY
   CRUST® Chocolate
   Pie Crust
½ cup chocolate syrup
   Whipped cream

1. Place large bowl in freezer. Mix peanut butter and honey in medium bowl. Place ice cream in bowl from freezer; add peanut butter mixture and cookies. Mix on low speed with electric mixer until blended.

2. Spoon half of ice cream mixture into crust. Spread chocolate syrup over ice cream mixture in crust. Spoon remaining ice cream mixture over chocolate syrup.

3. Garnish with whipped cream. Freeze leftovers.

makes 8 servings

prep time: 15 minutes

pudding poke cake

1 package (2-layer size)
   chocolate cake mix
   or cake mix with
   pudding in the mix
4 cups cold milk
2 packages (4-serving
   size) JELL-O®
   Vanilla Flavor
   Instant Pudding &
   Pie Filling

PREPARE and bake cake mix as directed on package for 13×9-inch baking pan. Remove from oven. Immediately poke holes down through cake to pan at 1-inch intervals with round handle of a wooden spoon. (Or poke holes with a plastic drinking straw, using turning motion to make large holes.)

POUR milk into large bowl. Add pudding mixes. Beat with wire whisk 2 minutes. Quickly pour about ½ of the thin pudding mixture evenly over warm cake and into holes. Let remaining pudding mixture stand to thicken slightly. Spoon over top of cake, swirling to frost cake.

REFRIGERATE at least 1 hour or until ready to serve.

makes 15 servings

preparation time: 30 minutes
baking time: 40 minutes
refrigerating time: 1 hour

mud slides

- **2 cups cold milk**
- **1 package (4-serving size) JELL-O® Chocolate Flavor Instant Pudding & Pie Filling**
- **14 chocolate sandwich cookies, finely crushed (about 1½ cups)**
- **2 cups thawed COOL WHIP® Whipped Topping**

LINE bottoms and sides of 2 loaf pans with wet paper towels. Tilt 2 (12-ounce) glasses in each pan.

POUR milk into 1-quart container with tight-fitting lid. Add pudding mix; cover tightly. Shake vigorously at least 45 seconds; pour evenly into glasses.

GENTLY stir 1¼ cups of the cookies into whipped topping with wire whisk in medium bowl until blended. Spoon evenly over pudding in glasses; sprinkle with remaining ¼ cup cookies.

REFRIGERATE until ready to serve.

makes 4 servings

cookies & cream cupcakes

- **2¼ cups all-purpose flour**
- **1 tablespoon baking powder**
- **½ teaspoon salt**
- **1⅔ cups sugar**
- **½ cup (1 stick) butter, softened**
- **1 cup milk**
- **2 teaspoons vanilla**
- **3 egg whites**
- **1 cup crushed chocolate sandwich cookies (about 10 cookies) plus additional for garnish**
- **1 container (16 ounces) vanilla frosting**

1. Preheat oven to 350°F. Line 24 regular-size (2½-inch) muffin pan cups with paper muffin cup liners.

2. Sift flour, baking powder and salt together in large bowl. Stir in sugar. Add butter, milk and vanilla; beat with electric mixer at low speed 30 seconds. Beat at medium speed 2 minutes. Add egg whites; beat 2 minutes. Stir in 1 cup crushed cookies.

3. Spoon batter into prepared muffin pans. Bake 20 to 25 minutes or until toothpick inserted into centers comes out clean. Cool in pans on wire racks 10 minutes. Remove to racks; cool completely.

4. Frost cupcakes; garnish with additional crushed cookies.

makes 24 cupcakes

mud slide

fudgy ripple cake

1 package
(18.25 ounces)
yellow cake mix
plus ingredients to
prepare mix

1 package (3 ounces)
cream cheese,
softened

2 tablespoons
unsweetened cocoa
powder

Fudgy Glaze (recipe
follows)

½ cup "M&M's"®
Chocolate Mini
Baking Bits

Preheat oven to 350°F. Lightly grease and flour 10-inch bundt or ring pan; set aside. Prepare cake mix as package directs. In medium bowl combine 1½ cups prepared batter, cream cheese and cocoa powder until smooth. Pour half of yellow batter into prepared pan. Drop spoonfuls of chocolate batter over yellow batter in pan. Top with remaining yellow batter. Bake about 45 minutes or until toothpick inserted near center comes out clean. Cool completely on wire rack. Unmold cake onto serving plate. Prepare Fudgy Glaze; spread over top of cake, allowing some glaze to run over side. Sprinkle with "M&M's"® Chocolate Mini Baking Bits. Store in tightly covered container.

makes 10 servings

fudgy glaze

1 square (1 ounce) semisweet chocolate
1 cup powdered sugar
⅓ cup unsweetened cocoa powder
3 tablespoons milk
½ teaspoon vanilla extract

Place chocolate in small microwave-safe bowl. Microwave at HIGH 30 seconds; stir. Repeat as necessary until chocolate is completely melted, stirring at 10-second intervals; set aside. In medium bowl combine powdered sugar and cocoa powder. Stir in milk, vanilla and melted chocolate until smooth.

double malted cupcakes

CUPCAKES

- 2 cups all-purpose flour
- ¼ cup malted milk powder
- 2 teaspoons baking powder
- ¼ teaspoon salt
- 1¾ cups granulated sugar
- ½ cup (1 stick) butter, softened
- 1 cup 2% or whole milk
- 1½ teaspoons vanilla
- 3 large egg whites

FROSTING

- 4 ounces milk chocolate candy bar, broken into chunks
- ¼ cup (½ stick) butter
- ¼ cup whipping cream
- 1 tablespoon malted milk powder
- 1 teaspoon vanilla
- 1¾ cups powdered sugar
- 30 chocolate-covered malt ball candies

1. Preheat oven to 350°F. Line 30 regular-size (2½-inch) muffin pan cups with paper muffin cup liners.

2. For cupcakes, combine flour, ¼ cup malted milk powder, baking powder and salt; mix well and set aside. Beat sugar and ½ cup butter with electric mixer at medium speed 1 minute. Add milk and 1½ teaspoons vanilla. Beat at low speed 30 seconds. Gradually beat in flour mixture; beat at medium speed 2 minutes. Add egg whites; beat 1 minute.

3. Spoon batter into prepared muffin cups filling ⅔ full. Bake 20 minutes or until golden brown and toothpick inserted into centers comes out clean. Cool in pans on wire racks 10 minutes. (Centers of cupcakes will sink slightly upon cooling.) Remove cupcakes to racks; cool completely. (At this point, cupcakes may be frozen up to 3 months.)

4. For frosting, melt chocolate and ¼ cup butter in heavy medium saucepan over low heat, stirring frequently. Stir in cream, 1 tablespoon malted milk powder and 1 teaspoon vanilla; mix well. Gradually stir in powdered sugar. Cook 4 to 5 minutes, stirring constantly, until small lumps disappear. Remove from heat. Chill 20 minutes, beating every 5 minutes until frosting is spreadable.

5. Spread cooled cupcakes with frosting; decorate with chocolate covered malt ball candies. Store at room temperature up to 24 hours or cover and refrigerate for up to 3 days before serving.

makes 30 cupcakes

290

291

crazy mixed-up bars

- 1 package (10 ounces) marshmallows
- 4 squares BAKER'S® Semi-Sweet Baking Chocolate, chopped
- 1 tub (8 ounces) COOL WHIP® Whipped Topping, thawed
- 1 package (13 ounces) POST® Cocoa *or* Fruity PEBBLES® Cereal

MICROWAVE marshmallows in large microwavable bowl on HIGH 1½ minutes until melted. Beat with wire whisk until smooth. Stir in chocolate until melted. Stir in whipped topping. Stir in cereal until well blended.

SPREAD mixture into foil-lined 13×9-inch pan sprayed with no-stick cooking spray. Freeze 4 hours or overnight.   *makes 20 bars*

fruity mixed-up bars: Substitute 4 squares BAKER'S White Chocolate Baking Squares for semi-sweet baking chocolate and Fruity PEBBLES Cereal for Cocoa PEBBLES; proceed as directed above.

prep time: 10 minutes

oatmeal raisin cookie pie

- 3 eggs
- 1 cup light corn syrup
- ½ cup packed brown sugar
- 3 tablespoons melted butter or margarine
- ¾ cup quick cooking oats
- ¾ cup raisins
- 1 tablespoon all-purpose flour
- 1 teaspoon ground cinnamon
- ¼ teaspoon salt
- 1 (6-ounce) READY CRUST® Graham Cracker Pie Crust
- Whipped cream or ice cream

1. Preheat oven to 325°F. Beat together eggs, corn syrup, sugar and butter. Add oats, raisins, flour, cinnamon and salt; mix well. Pour into crust.

2. Place on baking sheet and bake 45 to 50 minutes or until golden brown and filling is just set in center. Cool on wire rack.

3. Serve with whipped cream. Refrigerate leftovers.

makes 8 servings

prep time: 10 minutes
baking time: 45 minutes

fudge brownie pie

1 package (19 to 21 ounces) fudge brownie mix

1 cup cold milk

1 package (4-serving size) JELL-O® Chocolate Flavor Instant Pudding & Pie Filling

1 tub (8 ounces) COOL WHIP® Whipped Topping, thawed

PREPARE brownie mix as directed on package. Bake in greased 9-inch pie plate 40 minutes or until done according to doneness test on brownie package. Cool completely on wire rack.

SCOOP out center of brownie, using spoon, leaving 1-inch crust around edge and thin layer of brownie on bottom; reserve brownie scraps.

POUR milk into medium bowl. Add pudding mix. Beat with wire whisk until blended. Gently stir in half of the whipped topping and all but ¼ cup reserved brownie scraps. Spoon into center of crust. Top with remaining whipped topping and reserved ¼ cup brownie scraps.

REFRIGERATE 3 hours or until ready to serve. Garnish as desired.

makes 8 servings

prep time: 20 minutes

For an incredibly rich, extra-chocolatey dessert, garnish the pie with chocolate shavings, miniature chocolate chips and a light drizzle of hot fudge sauce.

frozen chocolate-covered bananas

2 ripe medium bananas

4 wooden sticks

½ cup low-fat granola cereal without raisins

⅓ cup hot fudge sauce, at room temperature

1. Line baking sheet or 15×10-inch jelly-roll pan with waxed paper.

2. Peel bananas; cut each in half crosswise. Insert wooden stick into center of cut end of each banana about 1½ inches into banana half. Place on prepared baking sheet; freeze until firm, at least 2 hours.

3. Place granola in large plastic food storage bag; crush slightly using rolling pin or meat mallet. Transfer granola to shallow plate. Place fudge sauce in a shallow dish.

4. Working with 1 banana at a time, place frozen banana in fudge sauce; turn banana and spread fudge sauce evenly onto banana with small rubber scraper. Immediately place banana on plate with granola; turn to coat lightly. Return to baking sheet in freezer. Repeat with remaining bananas.

5. Freeze until fudge sauce is very firm, at least 2 hours. Place on small plates; let stand 5 minutes before serving.   *makes 4 servings*

pudding in a cloud

2 cups COOL WHIP® Whipped Topping, thawed

2 cups cold milk

1 package (4-serving size) JELL-O® Instant Pudding & Pie Filling, any flavor

SPOON whipped topping evenly into 6 dessert dishes. Using back of spoon, make depression in center; spread whipped topping up side of each dish.

POUR milk into medium bowl. Add pudding mix. Beat with wire whisk 2 minutes. Let stand 5 minutes. Spoon pudding into center of whipped topping.

REFRIGERATE until ready to serve.   *makes 6 servings*

preparation time: 15 minutes
refrigerating time: 2 hours

creamy strawberry-orange pops

1 (8-ounce) container strawberry yogurt

¾ cup orange juice

2 teaspoons vanilla

2 cups frozen whole strawberries

1 packet sugar substitute or equivalent of 2 teaspoons sugar

6 (7-ounce) paper cups

6 wooden sticks

1. Combine yogurt, orange juice and vanilla in food processor or blender. Cover and blend until smooth.

2. Add frozen strawberries and sugar substitute. Blend until smooth. Pour into paper cups, filling each about ¾ full. Place in freezer for 1 hour. Insert wooden stick into center of each. Freeze completely. Peel cup off each to serve.

makes 6 servings

"m&m's"® brain freezer shake

2 cups any flavor ice cream

1 cup milk

¾ cup "M&M's"® Chocolate Mini Baking Bits, divided

Aerosol whipped topping

Additional "M&M's"® Chocolate Mini Baking Bits for garnish

In blender container combine ice cream and milk; blend until smooth. Add ½ cup "M&M's"® Chocolate Mini Baking Bits; blend just until mixed. Pour into 2 glasses. Top each glass with whipped topping; sprinkle with remaining ¼ cup "M&M's"® Chocolate Mini Baking Bits. Serve immediately.

makes 2 (1¼-cup) servings

peanut butter-banana brownie pizza

1 package (21½ ounces) brownie mix

1 package (8 ounces) PHILADELPHIA® Cream Cheese, softened

¼ cup sugar

¼ cup creamy peanut butter

3 large bananas, peeled, sliced

¼ cup coarsely chopped peanuts

2 squares BAKER'S® Semi-Sweet Chocolate

2 teaspoons butter or margarine

PREPARE brownie mix as directed on package. Spread batter evenly in greased 12-inch pizza pan. Bake 20 minutes. Cool completely on wire rack.

MIX cream cheese, sugar and peanut butter with electric mixer on medium speed until well blended. Spread over brownie. Arrange banana slices over cream cheese mixture; sprinkle with peanuts.

COOK chocolate and butter in heavy saucepan on very low heat, stirring constantly until just melted. Drizzle over bananas and peanuts.

makes 12 servings

prep time: 15 minutes
bake time: 20 minutes

frozen pudding cookiewiches™

1½ cups cold milk

½ cup peanut butter

1 package (4-serving size) JELL-O® Instant Pudding & Pie Filling, any flavor

24 graham crackers

Colored sprinkles

STIR milk gradually into peanut butter in deep narrow bottom bowl until smooth. Add pudding mix. Beat with wire whisk 2 minutes. Let stand 5 minutes.

SPREAD pudding mixture about ½-inch thick onto 12 of the crackers. Top with remaining crackers, pressing lightly and smoothing around edges with spatula. Coat edges with sprinkles.

FREEZE 3 hours or until firm.

makes 12 servings

preparation time: 15 minutes
freezing time: 3 hours

298

299

banana split cups

- 1 package (18 ounces) refrigerated chocolate chip cookie dough
- ⅔ cup "M&M's"® Chocolate Mini Baking Bits, divided
- 1 ripe medium banana, cut into 18 slices and halved
- ¾ cup chocolate syrup, divided
- 2¼ cups any flavor ice cream, softened
- Aerosol whipped topping
- ¼ cup chopped maraschino cherries

Lightly grease 36 (1¾-inch) mini muffin cups. Cut dough into 36 equal pieces; roll into balls. Place 1 ball in bottom of each muffin cup. Press dough onto bottoms and up sides of muffin cups; chill 15 minutes. Press ⅓ cup "M&M's"® Chocolate Mini Baking Bits into bottoms and sides of dough cups. Preheat oven to 350°F. Bake cookies 8 to 9 minutes. Cookies will be puffy. Remove from oven; gently press down center of each cookie. Return to oven 1 minute. Cool cookies in muffin cups 5 minutes. Remove to wire racks; cool completely. Place 1 banana half slice in each cookie cup; top with ½ teaspoon chocolate syrup. Place about ½ teaspoon "M&M's"® Chocolate Mini Baking Bits in each cookie cup; top with 1 tablespoon ice cream. Top each cookie cup with ½ teaspoon chocolate syrup, whipped topping, remaining "M&M's"® Chocolate Mini Baking Bits and 1 maraschino cherry piece. Store covered in freezer. *makes 3 dozen cookies*

wiggly giggly worms

- ½ cup boiling water
- 1 package (4-serving size) JELL-O® Gelatin Dessert, any flavor
- 1½ cups miniature marshmallows
- Small candies
- 8 chocolate wafer cookies, finely crushed (optional)

SPRAY 8-inch square pan with no-stick cooking spray. Stir boiling water into gelatin in medium microwavable bowl at least 2 minutes until completely dissolved.

ADD marshmallows; microwave on HIGH 1 minute until marshmallows are puffed and almost melted. Stir mixture slowly until marshmallows are completely melted and mixture is smooth. (Creamy layer will float to the top.) Pour into prepared pan.

REFRIGERATE 1 hour. Dip bottom of pan in warm water for 15 seconds. Loosen edges with a knife. Cut into 16 (½-inch) strips. Use candies for eyes on worms. Sprinkle cookie crumbs onto plate to resemble dirt. Place worms on top of dirt. *makes 16 worms*

prep time: 10 minutes
refrigerate time: 1 hour

mini cocoa cupcake kabobs

1 cup sugar

1 cup all-purpose flour

⅓ cup HERSHEY'S Cocoa

¾ teaspoon baking powder

¾ teaspoon baking soda

½ teaspoon salt

1 egg

½ cup milk

¼ cup vegetable oil

1 teaspoon vanilla extract

½ cup boiling water

Lickety-Split Cocoa Frosting (recipe follows)

Jelly beans or sugar nonpareils and/or decorating frosting

Marshmallows

Strawberries

Wooden skewers

1. Heat oven to 350°F. Spray small muffin cups (1¾ inches in diameter) with vegetable cooking spray.

2. Stir together sugar, flour, cocoa, baking powder, baking soda and salt in medium bowl. Add egg, milk, oil and vanilla; beat on medium speed of mixer 2 minutes. Stir in boiling water (batter will be thin). Fill muffin cups about ⅔ full with batter.

3. Bake 10 minutes or until wooden pick inserted in center comes out clean. Cool slightly; remove from pans to wire racks. Cool completely. Frost with Lickety-Split Cocoa Frosting. Garnish with jelly beans, nonpareils and/or white frosting piped onto cupcake. Alternate cupcakes, marshmallows and strawberries on skewers.

makes about 4 dozen cupcakes

lickety-split cocoa frosting: Beat 3 tablespoons softened butter or margarine in small bowl until creamy. Add 1¼ cups powdered sugar, ¼ cup HERSHEY'S Cocoa, 2 to 3 tablespoons milk and ½ teaspoon vanilla extract until smooth and of desired consistency. Makes about 1 cup frosting.

note: Number of kabobs will be determined by length of skewer used and number of cupcakes, marshmallows and strawberries placed on each skewer.

chocolate peanut butter parfaits

3 tablespoons milk

3 tablespoons peanut butter

1 cup thawed COOL WHIP® Whipped Topping

2 cups cold milk

1 package (4-serving size) JELL-O® Chocolate Flavor Instant Pudding & Pie Filling

¼ cup chopped peanuts

STIR 3 tablespoons milk into peanut butter in medium bowl until smooth. Gently stir in whipped topping.

POUR 2 cups milk into medium bowl. Add pudding mix. Beat with wire whisk 2 minutes. Alternately spoon whipped topping mixture and pudding into 6 parfait glasses.

REFRIGERATE until ready to serve. Sprinkle with peanuts.

makes 6 servings

preparation time: 5 minutes

frozen fudge pops

2 cups milk

⅓ cup honey*

3 tablespoons unsweetened cocoa powder

2 tablespoons cornstarch

1 teaspoon vanilla

1 teaspoon butter or margarine

Combine milk, honey, cocoa, cornstarch, vanilla and butter in medium saucepan. Cook and stir over low heat until little bubbles appear and mixture thickens. Remove from heat; cool slightly and pour into popsicle molds. Freeze 2 to 4 hours or until firm. Store in freezer.

makes 6 to 8 fudge pops

Favorite recipe from **National Honey Board**

Honey should not be fed to infants under one year of age. Honey is a safe and wholesome food for older children and adults.

applesauce cake

½ cup butter or margarine, softened

1 cup honey

1 egg

1 teaspoon vanilla

1¼ cups all-purpose flour

1 cup whole wheat flour

1 teaspoon baking soda

1 teaspoon ground cinnamon

½ teaspoon salt

½ teaspoon ground nutmeg

¼ teaspoon ground cloves

¼ teaspoon ground allspice or ginger

1 cup chopped dates

⅓ cup chopped walnuts

1 cup unsweetened applesauce

Cream butter in large bowl. Gradually beat in honey until light and fluffy. Add egg and vanilla; mix well. Combine dry ingredients in medium bowl; reserve 2 tablespoons flour mixture. Combine dates, walnuts and reserved 2 tablespoons flour mixture in small bowl; set aside. Add remaining flour mixture and applesauce alternately to creamed mixture, beginning and ending with flour mixture. Stir in date mixture. Pour batter into greased 13×9×2-inch pan. Bake at 325°F 35 minutes or until wooden pick inserted near center comes out clean.

makes 12 servings

Favorite recipe from **National Honey Board**

Chopped dried dates are available in packages at the supermarket. If you can't find them (or your child doesn't like them), raisins make a good substitute in many baked goods.

candy crunch pie

2 cups cold milk

2 packages (4-serving size each) JELL-O® Chocolate or Vanilla Flavor Instant Pudding & Pie Filling

1 tub (8 ounces) COOL WHIP® Whipped Topping, thawed, divided

4 bars (1.5 ounces each) chocolate-covered wafer candy bars, cut into ¼-inch pieces, divided

1 prepared chocolate-flavor crumb crust (6 ounces or 9 inches)

POUR milk into medium bowl. Add pudding mixes. Beat with wire whisk 1 minute or until well blended. (Mixture will be thick.) Gently stir in ½ of the whipped topping. Reserve ¼ cup of the candy bars. Stir remaining candy into pudding mixture. Spoon into crust.

SPREAD remaining whipped topping over pudding in crust. Sprinkle top with remaining candy.

REFRIGERATE 4 hours or until set.   *makes 8 servings*

how to: For best results, place candy bars in freezer or refrigerator prior to cutting.

great substitute: Substitute about 1 cup of your favorite candy bar (chopped) for the chocolate-covered wafer pieces.

note: If making pie in advance, reserve chopped candy bar pieces to garnish just before serving. This will prevent them from becoming soggy in refrigerator.

prep time: 5 minutes
refrigerate time: 4 hours

chocolate peanut butter cups

1 package DUNCAN HINES® Moist Deluxe® Swiss Chocolate Cake Mix

1 container DUNCAN HINES® Vanilla Frosting

½ cup creamy peanut butter

15 miniature peanut butter cup candies, wrappers removed, cut in half vertically

1. Preheat oven to 350°F. Place 30 (2½-inch) paper liners in muffin cups.

2. Prepare, bake and cool cupcakes following package directions for basic recipe.

3. Combine vanilla frosting and peanut butter in medium bowl. Stir until smooth. Frost one cupcake. Decorate with peanut butter cup candy, cut-side down. Repeat with remaining cupcakes and candies.

makes 30 servings

tip: You may substitute DUNCAN HINES® Moist Deluxe® Devil's Food, Dark Chocolate Fudge or Butter Recipe Fudge Cake Mix flavors for Swiss Chocolate Cake Mix.

fabulous fondue

1 cup semisweet chocolate chips

¼ cup 2% milk

2 to 3 tablespoons chopped pecans or walnuts

1 large banana, sliced

2 medium apples, sliced

2 medium oranges, peeled and cut into segments

1. Heat chocolate chips in small saucepan over very low heat until melted and smooth. Stir in milk and pecans; cook 1 minute.

2. Pour fondue into serving dish; serve immediately with fruit for dipping.

makes 6 servings (about 3 tablespoons fondue per serving)

tip: The possibilities for fondue dippers are endless! If fresh fruit is not available, try canned fruit or dried fruit. Cut a prepared pound cake or angel food cake into chunks for dipping, or set out a basket filled with a variety of small cookies.

308

brownie sundae cake

1 (19- to 21-ounce) package fudge brownie mix, prepared according to package directions for cake-like brownies

1 cup "M&M's"® Semi-Sweet Chocolate Mini Baking Bits

½ cup chopped nuts, optional

1 quart vanilla ice cream, softened

¼ cup caramel or butterscotch ice cream topping

Line 2 (9-inch) round cake pans with aluminum foil, extending slightly over edges of pans. Lightly spray bottoms with vegetable cooking spray; set aside. Preheat oven as brownie mix package directs. Divide brownie batter evenly between pans; sprinkle ½ cup "M&M's"® Semi-Sweet Chocolate Mini Baking Bits and ¼ cup nuts, if desired, over each pan. Bake 23 to 25 minutes or until edges begin to pull away from sides of pan. Cool completely. Remove layers by lifting foil from pans.

To assemble cake, place one brownie layer, topping-side down, in 9-inch springform pan. Carefully spread ice cream over brownie layer; drizzle with ice cream topping. Place second brownie layer on top of ice cream layer, topping-side up; press down lightly. Wrap in plastic wrap and freeze until firm. Remove from freezer about 15 minutes before serving. Remove side of pan. Cut into wedges.   *makes 12 slices*

fluffy banana pudding

3 cups cold milk

1 package (6-serving size) JELL-O® Banana Cream Flavor Instant Pudding & Pie Filling

1 tub (12 ounces) COOL WHIP® Whipped Topping, thawed

48 vanilla wafer cookies

3 bananas, sliced

POUR milk into large bowl. Add pudding mix. Beat with wire whisk 2 minutes. Let stand 5 minutes or until thickened. Gently stir in whipped topping.

PLACE 3 cookies and 3 or 4 banana slices in each of 8 dessert dishes. Top each with ½ cup pudding mixture; repeat layers. Garnish with additional whipped topping and cookies, if desired. Refrigerate until ready to serve.   *makes 8 servings*

prep time: 15 minutes

miniature cheesecakes

1 package (11.1 ounces) JELL-O® No Bake Real Cheesecake

2 tablespoons sugar

⅓ cup butter or margarine, melted

1½ cups cold milk

2 squares BAKER'S® Semi-Sweet Baking Chocolate, melted (optional)

MIX crumbs from mix, sugar and butter thoroughly with fork in medium bowl until crumbs are well moistened. Press onto bottoms of 12 paper-lined or foil-lined muffin cups.

BEAT milk and filling mix with electric mixer on low speed until blended. Beat on medium speed 3 minutes. (Filling will be thick.) Spoon over crumb mixture in muffin cups. Drizzle with melted chocolate, if desired.

REFRIGERATE at least 1 hour or until ready to serve. Garnish as desired. *makes 12 servings*

preparation time: 15 minutes
refrigerating time: 1 hour

chocolate chip cookie cake

1 package DUNCAN HINES® Moist Deluxe Yellow Cake Mix

1 (4-serving size) package vanilla-flavor instant pudding and pie filling mix

4 eggs

1 cup water

⅓ cup vegetable oil

1 (12-ounce) package semisweet chocolate chips

1½ cups finely chopped pecans

Confectioners' sugar for garnish

Preheat oven to 350°F. Grease and flour 10-inch Bundt pan.

Combine cake mix, pudding mix, eggs, water and oil in large mixing bowl. Beat at medium speed with electric mixer for 2 minutes. Stir in chips and pecans. Pour into prepared pan. Bake 50 to 60 minutes or until toothpick inserted in center comes out clean. Cool in pan 25 minutes. Invert onto serving plate. Cool completely. Dust with confectioners' sugar, if desired. *makes 12 to 16 servings*

microwave chocolate pudding

⅓ cup sugar

¼ cup unsweetened cocoa powder

2 tablespoons cornstarch

1½ cups reduced-fat (2%) milk

1 teaspoon vanilla

⅛ teaspoon ground cinnamon (optional)

Assorted small candies (optional)

1. Combine sugar, cocoa powder and cornstarch in medium microwavable bowl or 1-quart glass measure. Gradually add milk, stirring with wire whisk until well blended.

2. Microwave at HIGH 2 minutes; stir. Microwave at MEDIUM-HIGH (70% power) 3½ to 4½ minutes or until thickened, stirring every 1½ minutes.

3. Stir in vanilla and cinnamon, if desired. Let stand at least 5 minutes before serving, stirring occasionally to prevent skin from forming. Serve warm or chilled. Garnish with candies just before serving, if desired.

makes 4 (⅓-cup) servings

apple, caramel and nut roll-ups

½ cup chopped pecans

3 large Jonathan apples

1 tablespoon butter or margarine

¼ teaspoon ground nutmeg

¼ teaspoon ground cinnamon

6 (8-inch) thin flour tortillas

¾ cup caramel sauce

Whipped cream

1. Preheat oven to 300°F. Spread pecans in shallow baking pan. Bake 20 to 30 minutes or until lightly browned; set aside.

2. While toasting pecans, peel, core and slice apples. Place in microwavable container. Top with butter, nutmeg and cinnamon. Microwave, covered, on HIGH 3 minutes or until tender, stirring once; set aside. Place tortillas in plastic bag (do not seal). Microwave at HIGH 30 to 45 seconds or until heated through; set aside. Place caramel sauce in microwavable container. Microwave at HIGH 30 to 45 seconds or until hot.

3. Lay tortillas flat on work surface. Spoon ⅙ of apples down center of each tortilla. Top with 1 tablespoon nuts and 1 tablespoon sauce. Fold one side tortilla over filling; roll-up. Place on large serving platter or individual plates. Drizzle each roll-up with about 1 tablespoon sauce. Top with whipped cream and 1 teaspoon nuts. *makes 6 servings*

easy eclair dessert

27 whole graham crackers, halved

3 cups cold milk

2 packages (4-serving size) JELL-O® Vanilla Flavor Instant Pudding & Pie Filling

1 tub (12 ounces) COOL WHIP® Whipped Topping, thawed

1 container (16 ounces) ready-to-spread chocolate fudge frosting

Strawberries

ARRANGE ⅓ of the crackers on bottom of 13×9-inch baking pan, breaking crackers to fit, if necessary.

POUR milk into large bowl. Add pudding mixes. Beat with wire whisk 2 minutes. Gently stir in whipped topping. Spread ½ of the pudding mixture over crackers. Place ½ of the remaining crackers over pudding; top with remaining pudding mixture and crackers.

REMOVE top and foil from frosting container. Microwave frosting in container on HIGH 1 minute or until pourable. Spread evenly over crackers.

REFRIGERATE 4 hours or overnight. Cut into squares to serve. Garnish with strawberries. *makes 18 servings*

cool tips: You could make pistachio, banana-flavored or even double chocolate eclairs by simply changing the pudding flavors.

preparation time: 20 minutes
refrigerating time: 4 hours

This is an easy dessert for kids to help make—they can arrange the graham crackers in layers in the pan, stir up the pudding and even help spread the frosting on top.

316

easy eclair dessert

pretty in pink peppermint cupcakes

1 package (18.25 ounces) white cake mix

1⅓ cups water

3 large egg whites

2 tablespoons vegetable oil or melted butter

½ teaspoon peppermint extract

3 to 4 drops red liquid food coloring *or* ¼ teaspoon gel food coloring

1 container (16 ounces) prepared vanilla frosting

½ cup crushed peppermint candies (about 16 candies)

1. Preheat oven to 350°F. Line 30 regular-size (2½-inch) muffin pan cups with pink or white paper muffin cup liners.

2. Beat cake mix, water, egg whites, oil, peppermint extract and food coloring with electric mixer at low speed 30 seconds. Beat at medium speed 2 minutes.

3. Spoon batter into prepared cups filling ¾ full. Bake 20 to 22 minutes or until toothpick inserted into centers comes out clean. Cool in pans on wire racks 10 minutes. Remove cupcakes to racks; cool completely. (At this point, cupcakes may be frozen up to 3 months. Thaw at room temperature before frosting.)

4. Spread cooled cupcakes with frosting; top with crushed candies. Store at room temperature up to 24 hours or cover and refrigerate up to 3 days before serving. *makes about 30 cupcakes*

conversation heart cereal treats

2 tablespoons
  margarine or butter
20 large marshmallows
3 cups frosted oat
  cereal with
  marshmallow bits
12 large conversation
  hearts

1. Line 8- or 9-inch square pan with aluminum foil, leaving 2-inch overhangs on 2 sides. Generously grease or spray with nonstick cooking spray.

2. Melt margarine and marshmallows in medium saucepan over medium heat 3 minutes or until melted and smooth, stirring constantly. Remove from heat.

3. Add cereal; stir until completely coated. Spread in prepared pan; press evenly onto bottom using greased rubber spatula. Press heart candies into top of treats while still warm, evenly spacing to allow 1 heart per bar. Let cool 10 minutes. Using foil overhangs as handles, remove treats from pan. Cut into 12 bars. *makes 12 bars*

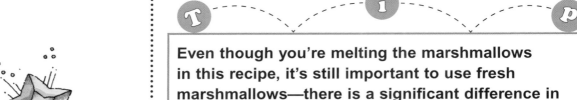

Even though you're melting the marshmallows in this recipe, it's still important to use fresh marshmallows—there is a significant difference in flavor between fresh and stale marshmallows.

To make this recipe even more appealing to kids, add a few drops of food coloring to the marshmallow mixture in the saucepan before stirring in the cereal.

320

shamrock ice cream sandwiches

**Butter Cookie Dough
(recipe follows)**

**3 or 4 drops green food
color**

**1 pint ice cream or
frozen yogurt,
any flavor**

1. Prepare cookie dough; mix in food color. Cover; refrigerate until firm, about 4 hours or overnight.

2. Preheat oven to 350°F.

3. Roll dough on lightly floured surface to ¼-inch thickness. Cut out cookies using 3½- to 5-inch shamrock-shaped cookie cutter. Place on ungreased cookie sheets.

4. Bake 8 to 10 minutes or until cookies are lightly browned around edges. Remove cookies to wire racks; cool completely.

5. Remove ice cream from freezer; let stand at room temperature to soften slightly, about 10 minutes. Spread 4 to 5 tablespoons ice cream onto flat sides of half the cookies. Place remaining cookies, flat sides down, on ice cream; press cookies together lightly.

6. Wrap each sandwich in foil; freeze until firm, about 2 hours or overnight.   *makes 6 to 8 cookie sandwiches*

note: Filled cookies store well up to 1 week in freezer.

butter cookie dough: Combine ¾ cup butter, softened, ¼ cup granulated sugar, ¼ cup packed light brown sugar and 1 egg yolk in medium bowl. Stir in 1¾ cups all-purpose flour, ¾ teaspoon baking powder and ⅛ teaspoon salt; mix well.

valentine ice cream sandwiches: Prepare and chill cookie dough as directed, substituting red food color for green food color. Cut out cookies with heart-shaped cookie cutter. Continue as directed.

patriotic ice cream sandwiches: Prepare and chill cookie dough as directed, substituting red food color for green food color. Cut out cookies with star-shaped cookie cutter. Continue as directed.

green's® lucky cake

1 package
    (18.25 ounces) any
    flavor cake mix, plus
    ingredients to
    prepare mix

½ teaspoon water

2 to 3 drops green food
    coloring

½ cup sweetened
    shredded coconut

6 tablespoons butter,
    softened

3¾ cups powdered sugar,
    divided

3 to 4 tablespoons milk

½ teaspoon vanilla

    Blue food coloring

1 cup "M&M's"®
    Chocolate Mini
    Baking Bits

Prepare and bake cake as directed on package for 13×9-inch cake. Cool cake completely on wire rack. In small bowl combine water and food coloring. Add coconut and stir until evenly tinted; set aside. In large bowl cream butter until light. Add 2 cups powdered sugar; beat until fluffy. Blend in 3 tablespoons milk and vanilla. Beat in remaining 1¾ cups powdered sugar until frosting is smooth. Add additional milk, 1 teaspoon at a time, if necessary to make frosting spreadable. Tint frosting desired shade of blue. Frost cake and decorate with tinted coconut and "M&M's"® Chocolate Mini Baking Bits as shown in photo.

makes 16 to 20 servings

st. patrick's parfaits

2 cups cold milk

1 package (4-serving
    size) JELL-O®
    Pistachio Flavor
    Instant Pudding
    & Pie Filling

    Chocolate sauce

2 cups thawed COOL
    WHIP® Whipped
    Topping

    Chocolate shamrock
    cutouts (optional)

POUR milk into large bowl. Add pudding mix. Beat with wire whisk 1 to 2 minutes.

LAYER pudding, chocolate sauce and 1 cup of the whipped topping alternately in 4 parfait glasses. Garnish with remaining whipped topping and chocolate shamrock cutouts.

REFRIGERATE until ready to serve.

makes 4 servings

festive easter cookies

1 cup butter, softened

2 cups powdered sugar

1 egg

2 teaspoons grated
lemon peel

1 teaspoon vanilla

3 cups all-purpose flour

½ teaspoon salt

Royal Icing (recipe
follows)

Assorted food colors

Assorted sprinkles
and candies

1. Beat butter and powdered sugar in large bowl at high speed of electric mixer until fluffy. Add egg, lemon peel and vanilla; mix well. Combine flour and salt in medium bowl. Add to butter mixture; mix well.

2. Divide dough in half. Wrap each half with plastic wrap. Refrigerate 3 hours or overnight.

3. Preheat oven to 375°F. Roll dough on floured surface to ⅛-inch thickness. Cut out dough using Easter cookie cutters, such as eggs, bunnies and tulips. Place cutouts on ungreased cookie sheets.

4. Bake 8 to 12 minutes or just until edges are very lightly browned. Remove to wire racks; cool completely. Prepare Royal Icing; tint with food colors as desired. Decorate with sprinkles and candies.

makes 4 dozen cookies

royal icing

1 egg white, at room temperature

2 to 2½ cups sifted powdered sugar

½ teaspoon almond extract

1. Beat egg white in small bowl with electric mixer at high speed until foamy. Gradually add 2 cups powdered sugar and almond extract. Beat at low speed until moistened. Increase mixer speed to high and beat until icing is stiff, adding additional powdered sugar if needed.

edible easter baskets

1 package (about 18 ounces) refrigerated sugar cookie dough

1 cup "M&M's"® Milk Chocolate Mini Baking Bits, divided

1 teaspoon water

1 to 2 drops green food coloring

¾ cup sweetened shredded coconut

¾ cup any flavor frosting

Red licorice whips, cut into 3-inch lengths

Lightly grease 36 (1¾-inch) mini muffin cups. Cut dough into 36 equal pieces; roll into balls. Place 1 ball in each muffin cup. Press dough onto bottom and up side of each muffin cup; chill 15 minutes. Press ⅓ cup "M&M's"® Milk Chocolate Mini Baking Bits into bottoms and sides of dough cups. Preheat oven to 350°F. Bake cookies 8 to 9 minutes. Cookies will be puffy. Remove from oven; gently press down center of each cookie. Return to oven 1 minute. Cool cookies in muffin cups 5 minutes. Remove to wire racks; cool completely. In medium bowl combine water and food coloring. Add coconut; stir until evenly tinted. In each cookie cup, layer 1 teaspoon frosting, 1 teaspoon tinted coconut and 1 teaspoon "M&M's"® Milk Chocolate Mini Baking Bits. Push both licorice ends into frosting to make basket handle. Store in tightly covered container.

makes 3 dozen cookies

328

easter hunt pie

1 (8-ounce) package cream cheese, softened

1 (14-ounce) can sweetened condensed milk

¾ cup cold water

1 (4-serving-size) package JELL-O® Vanilla Flavor Instant Pudding & Pie Filling Mix

1½ cups thawed COOL WHIP® Whipped Topping

1 (6-ounce) READY CRUST® Graham Cracker Pie Crust

16 miniature chocolate eggs or other holiday candies*

*For young children, use holiday marshmallow candies or other soft candies.

1. Beat cream cheese in large bowl until fluffy. Gradually beat in sweetened condensed milk until smooth. Add water and pudding mix; beat until smooth. Gently stir in whipped topping.

2. Spoon half of filling into crust. Place chocolate eggs evenly over filling. Top with remaining filling.

3. Chill 3 hours. Garnish as desired. Refrigerate leftovers.

makes 8 servings

prep time: 5 minutes
chilling time: 3 hours

To soften an 8-ounce package of cream cheese quickly and easily, remove it from the wrapper and place it on a microwavable plate. Heat at MEDIUM (50% power) for 15 to 20 seconds or just until it is slightly softened.

giant easter egg cookies

2 cups (4 sticks) butter or margarine, softened

½ cup granulated sugar

½ cup firmly packed light brown sugar

1 large egg

1 teaspoon vanilla extract

3½ cups all-purpose flour

½ teaspoon salt

1 cup chopped pecans

1¾ cups "M&M's"® Semi-Sweet Chocolate Mini Baking Bits, divided

Decorating icing in tubes

Preheat oven to 375°F. In large bowl cream butter and sugars until light and fluffy; beat in egg and vanilla. In medium bowl combine flour and salt; blend into creamed mixture. Stir in nuts and 1¼ cups "M&M's"® Semi-Sweet Chocolate Mini Baking Bits. Drop by ¼ cupfuls about 4 inches apart onto lightly greased cookie sheets; flatten each into egg shape about 4×2¾ inches. Bake 11 to 13 minutes or until lightly browned. Carefully remove to wire racks to cool completely. Decorate with icing and remaining ½ cup "M&M's"® Semi-Sweet Chocolate Mini Baking Bits. Store in tightly covered container.

makes about 2½ dozen cookies

easter basket cupcakes

24 Reynolds® Easter Bake Cups

1 package (about 18 ounces) white cake mix

1 container (16 ounces) white frosting

Flaked coconut

Green food color

Tiny jelly beans

Licorice twists

PREHEAT oven to 350°F. Place Reynolds Easter Bake Cups in muffin pans; set aside. Prepare cake mix following package directions for 24 cupcakes. Spoon batter into bake cups. Bake as directed. Cool.

FROST cupcakes; set aside.

TINT coconut green by mixing with food color. Make a coconut nest on top of each cupcake. Fill coconut nests with tiny jelly beans. For basket handles, with a knife, cut licorice twists in half lengthwise; cut halves into 6-inch pieces. Attach basket handles by inserting ends of licorice into cupcakes.

makes 24 cupcakes

chocolate bunny cookies

1 (21-ounce) package DUNCAN HINES® Family-Style Chewy Fudge Brownie Mix

1 egg

¼ cup water

¼ cup vegetable oil

1⅓ cups pecan halves (96)

1 container DUNCAN HINES® Dark Chocolate Fudge Frosting

Vanilla milk chips

1. Preheat oven to 350°F. Grease baking sheets.

2. Combine brownie mix, egg, water and oil in large bowl. Stir with spoon until well blended, about 50 strokes. Drop by 2 level teaspoonfuls 2 inches apart on greased baking sheets. Place two pecan halves, flat-side up, on each cookie for ears. Bake at 350°F 10 to 12 minutes or until set. Cool 2 minutes on baking sheets. Remove to cooling racks. Cool completely.

3. Spread Dark Chocolate Fudge frosting on one cookie. Place vanilla milk chips, upside down, on frosting for eyes and nose. Dot each eye with frosting using toothpick. Repeat for remaining cookies. Allow frosting to set before storing cookies between layers of waxed paper in airtight container.   *makes 4 dozen cookies*

tip: For variety, frost cookies with Duncan Hines® Vanilla Frosting and use semi-sweet chocolate chips for the eyes and noses.

chocolate bunny cookies

patriotic cocoa cupcakes

2 cups sugar

1¾ cups all-purpose flour

¾ cup HERSHEY'S Cocoa

2 teaspoons baking soda

1 teaspoon baking powder

1 teaspoon salt

2 eggs

1 cup buttermilk or sour milk*

1 cup boiling water

½ cup vegetable oil

1 teaspoon vanilla extract

Vanilla Frosting (recipe follows)

Chocolate stars or blue and red decorating icing (in tube)

*To sour milk: Use 1 tablespoon white vinegar plus milk to equal 1 cup.

1. Heat oven to 350°F. Grease and flour muffin cups (2½ inches in diameter) or line with paper bake cups.

2. Combine dry ingredients in large bowl. Add eggs, buttermilk, water, oil and vanilla; beat on medium speed of mixer 2 minutes (batter will be thin). Fill cups ⅔ full with batter.

3. Bake 15 minutes or until wooden pick inserted in center comes out clean. Remove cupcakes from pan. Cool completely. To make chocolate stars for garnish, if desired, cut several cupcakes into ½-inch slices; cut out star shapes from cake slices. Frost remaining cupcakes. Garnish with chocolate stars or with blue and red decorating icing.

makes about 30 cupcakes

vanilla frosting: Beat ¼ cup (½ stick) softened butter, ¼ cup shortening and 2 teaspoons vanilla extract. Add 1 cup powdered sugar; beat until creamy. Add 3 cups powdered sugar alternately with 3 to 4 tablespoons milk, beating to spreading consistency. Makes about 2⅓ cups frosting.

color-bright ice cream sandwiches

- ¾ cup (1½ sticks) butter or margarine, softened
- ¾ cup creamy peanut butter
- 1¼ cups firmly packed light brown sugar
- 1 large egg
- 1 teaspoon vanilla extract
- 1½ cups all-purpose flour
- 1 teaspoon baking soda
- ¼ teaspoon salt
- 1¾ cups "M&M's"® Chocolate Mini Baking Bits, divided
- 2 quarts vanilla or chocolate ice cream, slightly softened

Preheat oven to 350°F. In large bowl cream butter, peanut butter and sugar until light and fluffy; beat in egg and vanilla. In medium bowl combine flour, baking soda and salt; blend into creamed mixture. Stir in 1⅓ cups "M&M's"® Chocolate Mini Baking Bits. Shape dough into 1¼-inch balls. Place about 2 inches apart on ungreased cookie sheets. Gently flatten to about ½-inch thickness with fingertips. Place 7 or 8 of the remaining "M&M's"® Chocolate Mini Baking Bits on each cookie; press in lightly. Bake 10 to 12 minutes or until edges are light brown. *Do not overbake.* Cool about 1 minute on cookie sheets; cool completely on wire racks. Assemble cookies in pairs with about ⅓ cup ice cream; press cookies together lightly. Wrap each sandwich in plastic wrap; freeze until firm.

makes about 24 ice cream sandwiches

To soften a quart of rock-hard ice cream, microwave it at medium-low (30% power) for about 30 seconds. Test the softness with a knife before adding any additional time.

CELEBRATIONS

flag dessert

**2 pints fresh
strawberries**

**1 package (12 ounces)
pound cake, cut into
16 slices**

1⅓ cups blueberries

**1 tub (12 ounces) COOL
WHIP® Whipped
Topping, thawed**

SLICE 1 cup of the strawberries; set aside. Halve remaining strawberries; set aside.

LINE bottom of 12×8-inch glass baking dish with 8 cake slices. Top with 1 cup sliced strawberries, 1 cup of the blueberries and ½ of the whipped topping. Place remaining cake slices over whipped topping. Spread remaining whipped topping over cake. Arrange strawberry halves and remaining ⅓ cup blueberries over whipped topping to create a flag design.

REFRIGERATE until ready to serve.   *makes 15 servings*

star spangled snack

**1 package (4-serving
size) JELL-O® Brand
Berry Blue Flavor
Gelatin**

**1 package (4-serving
size) JELL-O® Brand
Gelatin, any red
flavor**

2 cups boiling water

1 cup cold water

**1 tub (8 ounces) COOL
WHIP® Whipped
Topping, thawed**

DISSOLVE each package of gelatin completely in 1 cup boiling water in separate bowls. Stir ½ cup cold water into each bowl of gelatin. Pour each mixture into separate 8-inch square pans. Refrigerate at least 3 hours or until firm. Cut gelatin in each pan into ½-inch cubes.

SPOON blue cubes evenly into 8 dessert dishes. Cover with whipped topping. Top with red cubes. Garnish with remaining whipped topping.

REFRIGERATE until ready to serve.   *makes 8 servings*

mummy dogs

**1 package
(8 breadsticks or
11 ounces)
breadstick dough**

**1 package (16 ounces)
hot dogs**

**Mustard and poppy
seeds**

• Preheat oven to 375°F. Using 1 dough strip for each, wrap hot dogs to look like mummies as shown in photo, leaving opening for eyes. Place on ungreased baking sheet.

• Bake 12 to 15 minutes or until light golden brown.

• Place dots of mustard and poppy seeds for eyes.

makes 8 servings

mini mummy dogs: Use 1 package (16 ounces) mini hot dogs instead of regular hot dogs. Cut each breadstick strip into 3 pieces. Cut each piece in half lengthwise. Using 1 strip of dough for each, wrap and bake mini hot dogs as directed above.

black cat cupcakes

**38 OREO® Chocolate
Sandwich Cookies,
divided**

**1 (18¼-ounce) package
devil's food cake
mix**

**1 (16-ounce) container
chocolate frosting**

Black string licorice

Jelly beans

**Semi-sweet chocolate
chips**

Black licorice whip

1. Coarsely chop 14 cookies. Prepare cake mix batter according to package directions; stir in chopped cookies. Spoon batter into 24 (2½-inch) paper-lined muffin cups.

2. Bake at 350°F for 20 minutes or until toothpick inserted in center comes out clean. Remove from pans; cool on wire rack.

3. Decorate the remaining 24 cookies using frosting to attach 4 (1½-inch) licorice strings for whiskers, 2 jelly bean halves for eyes and 2 chocolate chips for ears. Let set at least 30 minutes.

4. Frost cupcakes with remaining frosting. Stand cat faces on edge on each cupcake. Place 3-inch piece licorice whip on back half of each cupcake for tail.

makes 24 cupcakes

graveyard pudding dessert

3½ cups cold milk

2 packages (4-serving size) JELL-O® Chocolate Flavor Instant Pudding & Pie Filling

1 tub (12 ounces) COOL WHIP® Whipped Topping, thawed

1 package (16 ounces) chocolate sandwich cookies, crushed

Decorations: assorted rectangular-shaped sandwich cookies, decorator icings, candy corn and pumpkins

POUR milk into large bowl. Add pudding mixes. Beat with wire whisk or electric mixer on lowest speed 2 minutes or until blended. Gently stir in whipped topping and ½ of the crushed cookies. Spoon into 13×9-inch dish. Sprinkle with remaining crushed cookies.

REFRIGERATE 1 hour or until ready to serve. Decorate rectangular-shaped sandwich cookies with icings to make "tombstones." Stand tombstones on top of dessert with candies to resemble a graveyard.

makes 15 servings

preparation time: 15 minutes
refrigerating time: 1 hour

cheesy bat biscuits

1 can (16 ounces) jumbo refrigerated buttermilk biscuits

3 tablespoons butter, melted and divided

¼ cup grated Parmesan cheese

1 teaspoon dried parsley flakes

1 teaspoon dried basil leaves

• Preheat oven to 350°F.

• Flatten each biscuit into shape just large enough to fit 3-inch bat cookie cutter. Cut out bat shape; discard scraps. Place biscuits on baking sheet. Lightly score biscuits to outline bat wings; poke holes with toothpick for eyes. Brush biscuits with 1 tablespoon butter. Bake 7 minutes.

• Meanwhile, combine cheese, remaining 2 tablespoons butter, parsley and basil in small bowl.

• Turn biscuits on end and split into halves with fork. Spread 1 teaspoon cheese mixture on bottom half of each biscuit; replace biscuit top. Bake 3 minutes or until biscuits are golden brown. *makes 8 servings*

coffin cookies

1 package (18 ounces) refrigerated chocolate cookie dough*

Marshmallow Filling (recipe follows)

Colored sprinkles and sugars, prepared white icing and Halloween decors

If refrigerated chocolate cookie dough is unavailable, add ¼ cup unsweetened cocoa powder to refrigerated sugar cookie dough. Beat in large bowl until well blended.

- Draw pattern for coffin on cardboard; cut out pattern.

- Preheat oven to 350°F. Remove dough from wrapper according to package directions. Divide dough in half. Reserve 1 half; cover and refrigerate remaining half.

- Roll reserved dough on lightly floured surface to ⅛-inch thickness. Sprinkle with flour to minimize sticking, if necessary.

- Place pattern on cookie dough; cut dough around pattern with sharp knife. Repeat as necessary. Place cookies 2 inches apart on ungreased baking sheets. Repeat with remaining dough and scraps.

- Bake about 6 minutes or until firm but not browned. Cool on baking sheets 2 minutes. Remove to wire racks; cool completely.

- Prepare Marshmallow Filling. Spread half of cookies with 2 teaspoons filling each; top with remaining cookies. Roll cookie sandwich edges in sprinkles.

- Decorate with icing and assorted decors as desired.

makes about 2 dozen sandwich cookies

marshmallow filling: Combine 1 cup prepared vanilla frosting and ¾ cup marshmallow creme in small bowl until well blended.

345

scarecrow cupcakes

1¼ cups all-purpose flour

¾ teaspoon baking powder

½ teaspoon baking soda

¼ teaspoon salt

¾ teaspoon ground cinnamon

⅛ teaspoon ground cloves

⅛ teaspoon ground nutmeg

⅛ teaspoon ground allspice

¾ cup heavy cream

2 tablespoons molasses

¼ cup butter, softened

¼ cup granulated sugar

¼ cup packed brown sugar

2 eggs

½ teaspoon vanilla

¾ cup sweetened shredded coconut

Maple Frosting (recipe follows)

Toasted coconut, chow mein noodles, shredded wheat cereal, assorted candies and decorator gel

• Preheat oven to 350°F. Line 18 (2¾-inch) muffin cups with paper baking liners. Combine flour, baking powder, baking soda, salt and spices in medium bowl; set aside. Combine cream and molasses in small bowl; set aside.

• Beat butter in large bowl until creamy. Add granulated sugar and brown sugar; beat until light and fluffy. Add eggs, one at a time, beating well after each addition. Blend in vanilla.

• Add flour mixture alternately with cream mixture, beating well after each addition. Stir in coconut; spoon batter into prepared muffin cups, filling about half full.

• Bake 20 to 25 minutes or until toothpick inserted in centers comes out clean. Cool in pan on wire rack 10 minutes. Remove cupcakes to racks; cool completely.

• Prepare Maple Frosting. Frost cupcakes and decorate to make scarecrow faces as shown in photo. *makes 18 cupcakes*

maple frosting: Beat 2 tablespoons softened butter and 2 tablespoons maple or pancake syrup in medium bowl until well blended. Gradually beat in 1½ cups powdered sugar until smooth. Makes about 1½ cups.

ghostly delights

1 package (18 ounces) refrigerated cookie dough, any flavor

1 cup prepared vanilla frosting

¾ cup marshmallow creme

32 chocolate chips for decoration

1. Preheat oven to 350°F. Using about 1 tablespoon dough for body and about 1 teaspoon dough for head, form cookie dough into ghost shapes on greased cookie sheets. Bake 10 to 11 minutes or until browned. Cool 1 minute on cookie sheet; place warm cookies on serving plates.

2. While cookies are baking, combine frosting and marshmallow creme in small bowl until well blended.

3. Frost each ghost with frosting mixture. Press 2 chocolate chips, points up, into frosting mixture to create eyes on each ghost. Decorate with additional candy, if desired.   *makes 16 servings*

boo-tiful cupcakes

24 Reynolds® Halloween Bake Cups

1 package (about 18 ounces) cake mix

1 container (16 ounces) vanilla frosting

Orange food color

Halloween decorator sprinkles

1 cup premier white morsels

2 teaspoons shortening (not butter or margarine)

Cut-Rite® Wax Paper

PREHEAT oven to 350°F. Place Reynolds Halloween Bake Cups in muffin pans; set aside. Prepare cake mix following package directions for 24 cupcakes. Spoon batter into bake cups. Bake as directed. Cool.

TINT frosting with orange food color; frost cupcakes. Sprinkle with Halloween decorator sprinkles.

MELT premier white morsels following package directions. Add shortening; stir until melted. Spoon melted morsels into ghost shapes on cookie sheet lined with Cut-Rite Wax Paper. Add chocolate sprinkles for eyes. Refrigerate until firm. Stand one ghost in center of each cupcake.   *makes 24 cupcakes*

howlin' good party treats

1 (4-pack) individual serving vanilla pudding

Food coloring (orange=4 drops red plus 8 drops yellow; green=12 drops green)

1 (4-ounce) package READY CRUST® Mini-Graham Cracker Pie Crusts

FAMOUS AMOS® cookies, broken into pieces

Mini marshmallows

Toasted coconut

Candy corn

Colored sprinkles

Cinnamon candies

Black licorice

Mini semi-sweet chocolate chips

Mini baking bits

1. Mix pudding with food coloring. Divide pudding between crusts.

2. Decorate with pieces of Famous Amos® cookies and other toppings as desired. Refrigerate leftovers.

makes 6 servings

prep time: 5 minutes

Want to make your Halloween party a real scream? Try some of these ideas:

- Cut out scary decorations like cobwebs and bats and hang them from the ceiling.
- Play a recording of scary sounds to add to the spooky atmosphere.
- Create an eerie setting by replacing regular light bulbs with black, strobe or colored light bulbs and arranging fake cobwebs on and around the lamp shades to create menacing shadows.
- Serve beverages and snack mixes out of black plastic cauldrons, and be sure to cover your table with plenty of plastic spiders, skeletons and gummy worms.

350

turkey cupcakes

1 package (2-layer size) cake mix (any flavor) plus ingredients to prepare mix

1 container (16 ounces) chocolate frosting

¾ cup marshmallow creme

24 shortbread ring cookies

2 sticks white spearmint gum

48 small red candies

Candy corn and assorted candies for decoration

1. Preheat oven to 350°F. Line 24 regular-size (2½-inch) muffin cups with paper muffin cup liners.

2. Prepare cake mix according to package directions. Spoon batter into prepared muffin pans.

3. Bake 15 to 20 minutes or until wooden toothpick inserted into center comes out clean. Cool in pans on wire racks 10 minutes. Remove to racks; cool completely.

4. Combine frosting and marshmallow creme in medium bowl; mix well. Frost cupcakes lightly with frosting mixture; reserve remaining frosting mixture.

5. Cut cookies in half. Cut 24 halves in half again to form quarters.

6. For each cupcake, stand larger cookie piece upright on back edge of cupcake for tail. Place 1 of the 2 smaller cookie pieces on opposite side of cupcake for head; discard remaining smaller cookie piece or reserve for another use. Frost cookies with remaining frosting mixture so they blend in with cupcake.

7. Cut gum into ¼-inch pieces; trim both ends of gum into points. Fold gum in half to form beaks; place on bottom edges of heads. Position candies on heads for eyes. Decorate tops of tails with candies as desired.   *makes 2 dozen cupcakes*

gobble, gobble gobblers

½ cup (1 stick) butter, softened

½ cup granulated sugar

½ cup firmly packed light brown sugar

2 large eggs

2¼ cups all-purpose flour

1½ teaspoons ground cinnamon

1 teaspoon baking powder

½ teaspoon ground ginger

⅛ teaspoon ground cloves

½ cup vanilla frosting

½ cup chocolate frosting

1 cup "M&M's"® Chocolate Mini Baking Bits

In large bowl cream butter and sugars until light and fluffy; beat in eggs. In medium bowl combine flour, cinnamon, baking powder, ginger and cloves; add to creamed mixture. Wrap and refrigerate dough 2 to 3 hours. Preheat oven to 325°F. Lightly grease cookie sheets; set aside. Working with half the dough at a time on lightly floured surface, roll to ¼-inch thickness. Cut into turkey shapes using 3½-inch cookie cutters. Place about 2 inches apart on prepared cookie sheets. Bake 10 to 12 minutes. Cool 2 minutes on cookie sheets; cool completely on wire racks. In small bowl combine vanilla and chocolate frostings until well blended. Frost cookies and decorate with "M&M's"® Chocolate Mini Baking Bits. Store in tightly covered container.

makes 3 dozen cookies

christmas mouse ice creams

2 cups vanilla ice cream

1 package (4 ounces) single-serving graham cracker crusts

6 chocolate sandwich cookies, separated and cream filling removed

12 black jelly beans

6 red jelly beans

36 chocolate sprinkles (approximately ¼ teaspoon)

1. Place 1 rounded scoop (about ⅓ cup) ice cream into each crust. Freeze 10 minutes.

2. Press 1 cookie half into each side of ice cream scoops for ears. Decorate with black jelly beans for eyes, red jelly beans for noses and chocolate sprinkles for whiskers. Freeze 10 minutes.

makes 6 servings

T ----- i ----- P

If you're concerned about your kids eating too many sugary and/or fatty foods, especially during the holidays, simply substitute vanilla frozen yogurt for ice cream to make this a healthier dessert.

These simple desserts can be partially prepared ahead of time through step 1. Store the filled crusts in the freezer until just before you're ready to serve. Allow them to thaw slightly, then let the kids decorate the faces as shown in the photo.

354

yuletide twisters

1 (6-ounce) package premier white baking bars

4 teaspoons fat-free (skim) milk

4 teaspoons light corn syrup

8 ounces pretzel twists (about 80)

Cookie decorations, colored sugar or chocolate sprinkles

1. Line baking sheet with waxed paper; set aside.

2. Melt baking bars in small saucepan over low heat, stirring constantly. Stir in skim milk and corn syrup. Do not remove saucepan from heat.

3. Holding pretzel with fork, dip 1 side of each pretzel into melted mixture to coat. Place, coated side up, on prepared baking sheet; immediately sprinkle with desired decorations. Refrigerate until firm, 15 to 20 minutes. *makes 10 servings*

chocolate twisters: Substitute semisweet chocolate chips for premier white baking bars.

caramel dippity do's: Heat 1 cup caramel sauce and ⅓ cup finely chopped pecans in small saucepan until warm. Pour into small serving bowl. Serve with pretzels for dipping. Makes 8 servings (about 2 tablespoons each).

chocolate dippity do's: Heat 1 cup hot fudge sauce and ⅓ cup finely chopped pecans or walnuts in small saucepan until warm. Pour into small serving bowl. Serve with pretzels for dipping. Makes 8 servings (about 2 tablespoons each).

reindeer cupcakes

38 Holiday OREO® Chocolate Sandwich Cookies, divided

1 (18.25-ounce) package white cake mix with pudding

1¼ cups water

¼ cup vegetable oil

3 egg whites

48 mini pretzel twists

4 ounces white chocolate, melted

Red hot candies, white chocolate chips and miniature chocolate chips, for decorating

1 (16-ounce) can prepared chocolate frosting

1. Coarsely chop 14 cookies. Mix cake mix, water, oil and egg whites in large bowl with electric mixer at low speed until moistened. Beat 2 minutes at high speed. Stir in chopped cookies. Spoon batter into 24 paper-lined 2½-inch muffin-pan cups.

2. Bake at 350°F for 20 to 25 minutes or until toothpick inserted in center comes out clean. Remove from pans; cool on wire rack.

3. Cut a "V"-shaped portion off each remaining cookie to form reindeer face. Attach two pretzel twists to cookies using some melted chocolate for antlers. Decorate face using red hot candies and chocolate chips. Refrigerate until set.

4. To serve, frost cupcakes with chocolate frosting. Stand reindeer faces on edge on each cupcake.   *makes 24 cupcakes*

preparation time: 45 minutes
cook time: 20 minutes
cooling time: 1 hour
total time: 2 hours and 5 minutes

bunch o' balloons

- 1 package (20 ounces) refrigerated chocolate chip cookie dough
- 1 tub (8 ounces) COOL WHIP® Whipped Topping, thawed
- Assorted fruits and candies
- Decorating gel
- Red string licorice

HEAT oven to 350°F.

SLICE cookie dough evenly into 8 slices. Pat each slice into 5-inch circle on lightly floured surface. Place 2 inches apart on ungreased cookie sheets.

BAKE 10 to 12 minutes or until lightly browned. Remove from cookie sheets. Cool completely on wire racks.

SPREAD whipped topping evenly onto each cookie. Decorate with fruit, candy and gel. Arrange decorated cookies on large serving tray to resemble a bunch of balloons. Place a piece of licorice at bottom edge on each cookie to resemble string. Tie strings together with additional licorice. Serve immediately. *makes 8 servings*

clown cupcakes

- 1 package DUNCAN HINES® Moist Deluxe® Yellow Cake Mix
- 12 scoops vanilla ice cream
- 12 sugar ice cream cones
- 1 container (7 ounces) refrigerated aerosol whipped cream
- Assorted colored decors
- Assorted candies for eyes, nose and mouth

1. Preheat oven to 350°F. Place 2½-inch paper liners in 24 muffin cups.

2. Prepare, bake and cool cupcakes following package directions.

3. Remove paper from cupcakes. Place top-side down on serving plates. Top with scoops of ice cream. Place cones on ice cream for hats. Spray whipped cream around bottom of cupcakes for collars. Spray three small dots up front of cones. Sprinkle whipped cream with assorted colored decors. Use candies to make clowns' faces. *makes 12 clown cupcakes*

note: This recipe makes 24 cupcakes: 12 to make into "clowns" and 12 to freeze for later use.

360

play ball

- 2 cups plus
  1 tablespoon
  all-purpose flour,
  divided
- ¾ cup granulated sugar
- ¾ cup packed brown
  sugar
- 1 tablespoon baking
  powder
- 1 teaspoon salt
- ½ teaspoon baking soda
- ½ cup shortening
- 1¼ cups milk
- 3 eggs
- 1½ teaspoons vanilla
- ½ cup mini semisweet
  chocolate chips
- 1 container (16 ounces)
  vanilla frosting
- Assorted candies and
  food colorings

1. Preheat oven to 350°F. Line 24 regular-size (2½-inch) muffin pan cups with paper muffin cup liners.

2. Combine 2 cups flour, sugars, baking powder, salt and baking soda in medium bowl. Beat shortening, milk, eggs and vanilla with electric mixer at medium speed until well combined. Add dry ingredients; blend well. Beat at high speed 3 minutes, scraping side of bowl frequently. Toss mini chocolate chips with remaining 1 tablespoon flour; stir into batter. Divide evenly between prepared muffin cups.

3. Bake 20 minutes or until toothpick inserted into centers comes out clean. Cool in pan on wire racks 5 minutes. Remove cupcakes to racks; cool completely. Decorate with desired frostings and candies as shown in photo. *makes 24 cupcakes*

For kids who love sports, these cupcakes make the perfect party treat! You can create a variety, such as baseball, basketball and soccer balls; or, if you're inviting the whole team over, just make whatever cupcake fits the sport. Party supply stores carry lots of sports-themed paper plates, cups, napkins and party favors, so putting together this party should be a breeze.

sweet holidays pizza

CELEBRATIONS

Sweet Crumb Crust
(recipe follows)

1½ pints (3 cups) vanilla
or other desired
flavor frozen yogurt,
slightly softened

1½ pints (3 cups)
chocolate or other
desired flavor frozen
yogurt, slightly
softened

1 cup canned or fresh
pineapple chunks

6 whole fresh
strawberries,
cut in half

1 cup thawed frozen
peach slices or
1 medium peach,
peeled and sliced

1 kiwi, peeled and sliced

12 pecan halves
(optional)

¼ cup chocolate syrup,
heated chocolate
fudge sauce or
favorite fruit-
flavored ice cream
topping

1. Prepare Sweet Crumb Crust.

2. Spread yogurts onto crust to within ½ inch of edge. Cover with plastic wrap; freeze until firm, 6 hours or overnight.

3. Arrange fruits and nuts decoratively on top of pizza just before serving. Drizzle with chocolate syrup. Cut into wedges to serve.

makes 16 servings

sweet crumb crust: Line 12-inch pizza pan with aluminum foil. Combine 2 cups graham cracker or vanilla wafer cookie crumbs, ¼ cup sugar and ¾ teaspoon ground cinnamon in medium bowl; stir in 6 tablespoons melted butter. Press mixture evenly onto bottom of prepared pan. Freeze 15 minutes.

rocky road pizza: Omit vanilla frozen yogurt and fruits. Increase chocolate frozen yogurt to 1½ quarts (6 cups). Substitute 3 tablespoons chopped dry roasted peanuts for pecan halves. Prepare crust as directed. Spread yogurt onto crust as directed; cover and freeze until firm. Sprinkle with ¾ cup miniature marshmallows. Drizzle with chocolate syrup.

sweet valentine pizza: Omit chocolate syrup. Prepare crust as directed. Substitute 1½ quarts (6 cups) strawberry frozen yogurt for the chocolate and vanilla frozen yogurts, and ½ to ¾ cup halved fresh strawberries for assorted fresh fruits. Drizzle with chocolate syrup or strawberry ice cream topping.

365

captivating caterpillar cupcakes

1 package DUNCAN HINES® Moist Deluxe® White Cake Mix

3 egg whites

1⅓ cups water

2 tablespoons vegetable oil

½ cup star decors, divided

1 container DUNCAN HINES® Vanilla Frosting

Green food coloring

6 chocolate sandwich cookies, finely crushed (see Tip)

½ cup candy-coated chocolate pieces

⅓ cup assorted jelly beans

Assorted nonpareil decors

1. Preheat oven to 350°F. Place 24 (2½-inch) paper liners in muffin cups.

2. Combine cake mix, egg whites, water and oil in large bowl. Beat at low speed with electric mixer until moistened. Beat at medium speed 2 minutes. Fold in ⅓ cup star decors. Fill paper liners about half full. Bake at 350°F 18 to 23 minutes or until toothpick inserted in center comes out clean. Cool in pans 5 minutes. Remove to cooling racks. Cool completely.

3. Tint vanilla frosting with green food coloring. Frost one cupcake. Sprinkle ½ teaspoon chocolate cookie crumbs on frosting. Arrange 4 candy-coated chocolate pieces to form caterpillar body. Place jelly bean at one end to form head. Attach remaining star and nonpareil decors with dots of frosting to form eyes. Repeat with remaining cupcakes. *makes 24 cupcakes*

tip: To finely crush chocolate sandwich cookies, place cookies in resealable plastic bag. Remove excess air from bag; seal. Press rolling pin on top of cookies to break into pieces. Continue pressing until evenly crushed.

easy celebration ice cream cake

- **10 chocolate wafer cookies**
- **1 pint (2 cups) ice cream, any flavor, softened**
- **1 jar (16 ounces) chocolate fudge sauce**
- **3 packages (2.07 ounces each) chocolate-covered caramel peanut nougat bars, chopped**
- **1 tub (8 ounces) COOL WHIP® Whipped Topping, thawed**

LINE 9-inch round cake pan with plastic wrap. Arrange cookies in bottom of pan. Spread ice cream over cookies. Reserve ½ cup fudge sauce. Pour remaining fudge sauce over ice cream.

MIX candy into whipped topping. Spread whipped topping mixture over fudge sauce in pan. Drizzle with reserved fudge sauce.

FREEZE 4 hours or overnight. Lift cake out of pan; peel off plastic wrap. Let stand 10 minutes. Top with additional candy, if desired.

makes 10 servings

cool whip® fun fact: The COOL WHIP® brand name is recognized by 99% of Americans.

prep time: 15 minutes

frizzy the clown cupcakes

- **24 Reynolds® Bake Cups**
- **1 package (about 18 ounces) cake mix**
- **1 container (16 ounces) vanilla frosting**
- **Orange food coloring**
- **Powdered sugar**
- **12 gummy fruit-flavored ring candies**
- **24 small gumdrops**
- **48 mini candy-coated plain chocolate candies**
- **Red string licorice**

PREHEAT oven to 350°F. Place Reynolds Bake Cups in muffin pans; set aside. Prepare cake mix following package directions for 24 cupcakes. Spoon batter into bake cups. Bake as directed. Cool.

FROST cupcakes; set aside.

TINT a small amount of frosting with orange food coloring for Frizzy's hair. Add powdered sugar to frosting until it is no longer sticky (has consistency of cookie dough). Press frosting through garlic press or fine strainer. Pinch strands of frosting together and press on cupcake. For mouth, cut section of gummy fruit-flavored ring candy; add to cupcake. Add gumdrop for nose, chocolate candies for eyes and red string licorice for eyebrows.

makes 24 cupcakes

367

s'mores on a stick

1 (14-ounce) can EAGLE® BRAND Sweetened Condensed Milk (NOT evaporated milk)

1½ cups milk chocolate mini chips, divided

1 cup miniature marshmallows

11 whole graham crackers, halved crosswise

Toppings: chopped peanuts, mini candy-coated chocolate pieces, sprinkles

1. Microwave half of Eagle Brand in microwave-safe bowl on HIGH (100% power) 1½ minutes. Stir in 1 cup chocolate chips until smooth; stir in marshmallows.

2. Spread evenly by heaping tablespoonfuls onto 11 graham cracker halves. Top with remaining graham cracker halves; place on waxed paper.

3. Microwave remaining Eagle Brand on HIGH (100% power) 1½ minutes; stir in remaining ½ cup chocolate chips, stirring until smooth. Drizzle mixture over cookies and sprinkle with desired toppings.

4. Let stand for 2 hours; insert a wooden craft stick into center of each cookie. *makes 11 servings*

prep time: 10 minutes
cook time: 3 minutes

old-fashioned pop corn balls

2 quarts popped JOLLY TIME® Pop Corn

1 cup sugar

⅓ cup light or dark corn syrup

⅓ cup water

¼ cup butter or margarine

½ teaspoon salt

1 teaspoon vanilla

Keep popped pop corn warm in 200°F oven while preparing syrup. In 2-quart saucepan, stir together sugar, corn syrup, water, butter and salt. Cook over medium heat, stirring constantly, until mixture comes to a boil. Continue cooking without stirring until temperature reaches 270°F on candy thermometer or until small amount of syrup dropped into very cold water separates into threads which are hard but not brittle. Remove from heat. Add vanilla; stir just enough to mix through hot syrup. Slowly pour over popped pop corn, stirring to coat well. Cool just enough to handle. With JOLLY TIME® Pop Corn Ball Maker or buttered hands, shape into balls. *makes 12 medium-sized pop corn balls*

368

ice cream cone cakes

1 package (18¼ ounces) devil's food cake mix plus ingredients to prepare mix

⅓ cup sour cream

1 package (2⅝ ounces) flat-bottomed ice cream cones (about 18 cones)

1¼ cups nonfat frozen yogurt (any flavor)

Cake decorations or chocolate sprinkles

1. Preheat oven to 350°F. Grease and flour 8- or 9-inch round cake pan; set aside.

2. Prepare cake mix according to package directions, substituting sour cream for ⅓ cup of the water and decreasing oil to ¼ cup.

3. Spoon ½ of the batter (about 2⅓ cups) evenly into ice cream cones, using about 2 tablespoons batter for each. Pour remaining batter into prepared cake pan.

4. Stand cones on cookie sheet. Bake cones and cake layer until toothpick inserted into center of cake comes out clean, about 20 minutes for cones and about 35 minutes for cake layer. Cool on wire racks, removing cake from pan after 10 minutes. Reserve or freeze cake layer for another use.

5. Top each filled cone with ¼ cup scoop of frozen yogurt just before serving. Sprinkle with decorations as desired. Serve immediately.

makes 18 servings

These ice cream cone cakes are versatile desserts that can adapt well to any holiday or occasion. Use vanilla frozen yogurt or ice cream with pink decorations for Valentine's Day, strawberry frozen yogurt with blue and white decorations for the 4th of July, and chocolate frozen yogurt with orange decorations for Halloween.

371

fudge cheesecake bars

4 bars (1 ounce *each*) HERSHEY'S Unsweetened Baking Chocolate, broken into pieces

1 cup (2 sticks) butter or margarine

2½ cups sugar, divided

4 eggs

1 teaspoon vanilla extract

2 cups all-purpose flour

1 package (8 ounces) cream cheese, softened

1 package (13 ounces) HERSHEY'S HUGS Chocolates *or* HUGS WITH ALMONDS Chocolates, divided

1. Heat oven to 350°F. Grease 13×9×2-inch baking pan.

2. Place baking chocolate and butter in large microwave-safe bowl. Microwave at HIGH (100%) 2 to 2½ minutes, or until butter and chocolate are completely melted, stirring after each minute. Beat in 2 cups sugar, 3 eggs and vanilla until blended. Stir in flour; spread batter into prepared pan.

3. Beat cream cheese, remaining ½ cup sugar and remaining 1 egg in small bowl until blended. Remove wrappers from 12 chocolate pieces. Coarsely chop; stir into cream cheese mixture. Drop batter by spoonfuls over top of chocolate mixture in pan. Swirl with knife for marbled effect.

4. Bake 35 to 40 minutes or just until set. Cool completely in pan on wire rack. Cut into bars. Remove wrappers from remaining chocolate pieces; press onto tops of bars. Cover; refrigerate leftover bars.

makes about 3 dozen bars

peanut butter treats

1¼ cups firmly packed light brown sugar

¾ Butter Flavor CRISCO® Stick or ¾ cup Butter Flavor CRISCO® all-vegetable shortening

2 tablespoons milk

1 tablespoon vanilla

1 egg

1¾ cups all-purpose flour

1 teaspoon salt

¾ teaspoon baking soda

2 cups (about 32) miniature peanut butter cups, unwrapped and quartered or coarsely chopped

1. Heat oven to 375°F. Place sheets of foil on countertop for cooling cookies.

2. Place brown sugar, shortening, milk and vanilla in large bowl. Beat at medium speed of electric mixer until well blended. Add egg; beat well.

3. Combine flour, salt and baking soda. Add to shortening mixture; beat at low speed just until blended. Stir in peanut butter cup quarters.

4. Drop dough by rounded measuring tablespoonfuls 3 inches apart onto *ungreased* baking sheets.

5. Bake one baking sheet at a time at 375°F for 8 to 10 minutes or until cookies are lightly browned. *Do not overbake.* Cool 2 minutes on baking sheet. Remove cookies to foil to cool completely.

makes about 3 dozen cookies

ACKNOWLEDGMENTS

The publishers would like to thank the companies and organizations listed below for the use of their recipes and photographs in this publication.

Bestfoods

Birds Eye®

Bob Evans®

ConAgra Grocery Products Company

Del Monte Corporation

Dole Food Company, Inc.

Domino Sugar Corporation

Duncan Hines® and Moist Deluxe® are registered trademarks of Aurora Foods Inc.

Eagle® Brand

Egg Beaters®

The Golden Grain Company®

Grandma's® is a registered trademark of Mott's, Inc.

Hebrew National®

Hershey Foods Corporation

Hillshire Farm®

HONEY MAID® Honey Grahams

The HV Company

JOLLY TIME® Pop Corn

Keebler® Company

Kellogg Company

Kraft Foods Holdings

Lawry's® Foods, Inc.

©Mars, Inc. 2001

Nabisco Biscuit Company

National Honey Board

Nestlé USA, Inc.

New York Apple Association, Inc.

NILLA® Wafers

OREO® Chocolate Sandwich Cookies

Peanut Advisory Board

Perdue Farms Incorporated

PLANTERS® Nuts

The Procter & Gamble Company

The Quaker® Oatmeal Kitchens

Reckitt Benckiser

Reynolds Metals Company

Sargento® Foods Inc.

The J.M. Smucker Company

StarKist® Seafood Company

The Sugar Association, Inc.

Texas Peanut Producers Board

Tyson Foods, Inc.

Unilever Bestfoods North America

Wisconsin Milk Marketing Board

INDEX

375

METRIC CONVERSION CHART

VOLUME MEASUREMENTS (dry)

1/8 teaspoon = 0.5 mL
1/4 teaspoon = 1 mL
1/2 teaspoon = 2 mL
3/4 teaspoon = 4 mL
1 teaspoon = 5 mL
1 tablespoon = 15 mL
2 tablespoons = 30 mL
1/4 cup = 60 mL
1/3 cup = 75 mL
1/2 cup = 125 mL
2/3 cup = 150 mL
3/4 cup = 175 mL
1 cup = 250 mL
2 cups = 1 pint = 500 mL
3 cups = 750 mL
4 cups = 1 quart = 1 L

VOLUME MEASUREMENTS (fluid)

1 fluid ounce (2 tablespoons) = 30 mL
4 fluid ounces (1/2 cup) = 125 mL
8 fluid ounces (1 cup) = 250 mL
12 fluid ounces (1 1/2 cups) = 375 mL
16 fluid ounces (2 cups) = 500 mL

WEIGHTS (mass)

1/2 ounce = 15 g
1 ounce = 30 g
3 ounces = 90 g
4 ounces = 120 g
8 ounces = 225 g
10 ounces = 285 g
12 ounces = 360 g
16 ounces = 1 pound = 450 g

DIMENSIONS

1/16 inch = 2 mm
1/8 inch = 3 mm
1/4 inch = 6 mm
1/2 inch = 1.5 cm
3/4 inch = 2 cm
1 inch = 2.5 cm

OVEN TEMPERATURES

250°F = 120°C
275°F = 140°C
300°F = 150°C
325°F = 160°C
350°F = 180°C
375°F = 190°C
400°F = 200°C
425°F = 220°C
450°F = 230°C

BAKING PAN SIZES

Utensil	Size in Inches/Quarts	Metric Volume	Size in Centimeters
Baking or Cake Pan (square or rectangular)	8×8×2	2 L	20×20×5
	9×9×2	2.5 L	23×23×5
	12×8×2	3 L	30×20×5
	13×9×2	3.5 L	33×23×5
Loaf Pan	8×4×3	1.5 L	20×10×7
	9×5×3	2 L	23×13×7
Round Layer Cake Pan	8×1½	1.2 L	20×4
	9×1½	1.5 L	23×4
Pie Plate	8×1¼	750 mL	20×3
	9×1¼	1 L	23×3
Baking Dish or Casserole	1 quart	1 L	—
	1½ quart	1.5 L	—
	2 quart	2 L	—